LETTERS from TEXAS

2021-2023

by

E. R. BILLS

Fort Worth, Texas

STARKWEATHER IMPRINTS

Copyright © 2024
Cover Art by E. R. Bills
Cover Design by E. R. Bills

STARKWEATHER IMPRINTS
P.O. Box 10553
River Oaks, Texas 76114

All rights reserved.

No part of this book may be reproduced in any form or by any electronic or mechanical means, including information storage and retrieval systems, without specifically expressed, written consent from the author, except for the use of brief quotations in a book review.

*Strict censorship is the thing that will bring the honest truth.
That is what we are working for and that is what we are
going to have.*

—Mrs. M.M. Birge, Chairwoman of the Textbook
Committee, Proceedings of the Twentieth Annual
Convention of the Texas Division, United
Daughters of the Confederacy (1915)

PRAISE FOR E.R BILLS

Tell-Tale Texas: Investigations in Infamous History
An award-winning freelance journalist and author of multiple books on Texas history, Bills has a firm grasp on the state's past and its warped self-perception, and he bolsters his analysis with more than 100 endnotes and a nine-page bibliography. The book's lack of a chronological throughline (and jumps between multiple time periods within each chapter) may be dizzying to some readers, but overall, the text balances sound research with a harrowing narrative and biting commentary. Ample photographs and newspaper clippings further immerse readers in the milieu. Texas history is also used as a lens through which the author explores larger trends in the American story; each chapter features historical figures like Martin Luther King Jr. or Ida B. Wells, who link events in Texas to a larger narrative of American anti-immigrant sentiment, white supremacy, and racial discrimination. "Sometimes, when you confront the past," he warns readers, "the past confronts you back." A searing indictment of racism in Texas, past and present. –***Kirkus Reviews*, August 7, 2023**

The San Marcos 10: An Antiwar Protest in Texas
Fifty years ago at sleepy Southwest Texas State University (now Texas State University), many of society's complex conflicts aligned in what became known as the San Marcos 10. The story was mostly forgotten-- until now . . . E. R. Bills takes the reader on another journey in this book. Free speech, civil rights, justice, poverty, dress codes, the Vietnam War and abuses of power are masterfully explored at a national level through the detail of experiences taking place in San Marcos. –***The Galveston Daily News*, November 9, 2019**

Texas Oblivion: Mysterious Disappearances, Escapes and Cover-Ups
Bills' volume harkens back to an earlier, pulpier era of paperback true crime. His prose style is lean and matter-of-fact, though he knows how to give each narrative a satisfying shape—no easy feat when the mysteries are never solved . . . Authoritative and well-researched, the stories are enthralling not only for their enigmatic natures, but also for the colorful picture they paint of Texas: its history, its culture, and the

ways its crimes get investigated (or not). The book is the perfect read for a plane ride or beach day—preferably one in the Lone Star State. A varied and well-crafted assemblage of missing person accounts.
–Kirkus Reviews, **August 20, 2021**

A voice for the forgotten. *–Texas Books in Review*, **Fall 2021**

The 1910 Slocum Massacre: An Act of Genocide in East Texas
Bills follows the lead of a number of students of racial violence who have sought to restore historical memory to communities where incidents of racial violence are seldom spoken about . . . For Bills, substantive efforts toward racial reconciliation in post-James Byrd[1] Texas, similar to the proactive steps taken in the past decade in Rosewood and Tulsa, mark the only hope for Texans, southerners and all Americans to remedy the ongoing racial tensions that confront the United States. This volume, accessible to both scholarly and general audiences interested in the history of racial violence, African American history, and Texas history, seeks to assist in that ambitions goal."
–Journal of Southern History, **August 2015, Vol. LXXXI, No. 3, p. 756-757.**

CONTENTS

ACKNOWLEDGEMENTS

Special thanks to all the publications and websites that have published my columns and editorials over the years, especially and more recently, *Fort Worth Weekly* and *Dissident Voice*.

INTRODUCTION

I have been writing letters to, for, and concerning my fellow Texans, on and off, for about thirty-five years. It's been a mostly thankless and arguably imprudent effort that has won me less friends than foes, and earned more death threats than awards. These editorials may be exercises in futility and vanity, but here Albert Camus bails me out. "This undertaking, I know, cannot be accomplished without dangers and bitterness. We must accept the dangers: the era of chairbound artists is over. But we must reject bitterness. One of the temptations of an artist is to believe himself solitary … But this is not true. He stands in the midst of all, the same rank, neither higher nor lower, with all those who are working and struggling. His very vocation, in the face of oppression, is to open the prisons and to give a voice to the sorrows and joys of all. This is where art, against its enemies, justifies itself by proving precisely that it is no one's enemy."

The enemy is obviousness and it is relentlessly formidable. I have come to suspect that wars that can undoubtedly be won are hardly worth fighting, and that real bravery lies in participating in seemingly unwinnable battles. It was never my aim to live on one of the frontlines; but our historical moment is beset by unavoidable conflicts in which the victors are rarely if ever admirable or credible, especially here in Texas. So, we become Camus' Sisyphus, dutifully placing our shoulder to the stone and heartened by meaningful toil. Apologies, beforehand, for redundances.

E. R.
January 1, 2024

Handmaid Tells

Those who know, know.

Those who don't know, need to be told

I am infected. I am a carrier.

I am contagious.

I didn't realize it myself, at first. And then, when I became aware, I was afraid. It made me different. I wanted to hide it. I tried to hide it. I wasn't sure I wanted anyone else to know. I didn't know what they would think.

It wasn't my fault, really. I was exposed at a very young age.

I had no idea what I had contracted. And by the time I understood, it was too late. I never completely recovered. It spread through my existence like a wildfire, and I was horrified by the implications.

Early on, I averted my eyes and tried to conceal the truth. I wanted to be normal and fit in. But I couldn't. And I didn't know it then, but I never would.

I was sick and that was the end of it, and certainly the end of any real, normal beginning. A normal life. Commonality with most of those around me. Even some that I loved. As I grew older, my condition grew worse, but it became more manageable. I was more realistic. I learned to accept the presence of the contagion. I had to accept the finality of my condition, and I eventually did. And I'm glad I did. Even now, when people like me are being quarantined.

I was reading a book called *If It Bleeds*.[2] I was no longer looking for answers or a cure for my condition. Or even an

A "Librarian Bomber" about to hurl Margaret Atwood's The Handmaid's Tale. Wikipedia Commons.[3]

articulation of my affliction. The malaise that defined my existence, practically for as long as I could remember. It affected me in unexpected ways and changed the trajectory of my life. It was a sentence to be served.

I was reading *If It Bleeds*, and a line jumped out. It surprised me and I read it again. And then I read it out loud.

"A reader is a carrier, not a creator."

A reader is a carrier, not a creator.

I had been, and still was, a carrier.

I was exposed to multiple strains of the contagion very early. I couldn't list them all. I remember *The Great Brain* series by John D. Fitzgerald.[4] I remember *The Count of Monte Cristo* by Alexander Dumas. Bob Dylan. Edgar Rice Burroughs. *Frankenstein* by Mary Shelley. Joseph Conrad. Franza Kafka. Herman Melville. Hemingway. F. Scott Fitzgerald. Tolkien. Henry Miller, Shakespeare. Poe. H.G. Wells. Joseph Heller. *National Defense* by James Fallows. Albert Camus, Nietzsche. *1984*—George Orwell. *The Heart is a Lonely Hunter* by Carson McCullers. Flannery O'Connor.[5] Plato. Steinbeck.

Steinbeck.

In 1987, I remember sitting in a Texas State University honors course called "Science Fiction and Society." We were assigned a book to read before each class and the whole course was mostly just meeting once a week to discuss each reading. A few lectures. I don't recall an exam. Maybe one or two papers. I can't remember the professor's name. Maybe Deduck. Dr. Deduck. She had been afflicted as well. When she was young, she and a friend went looking for John Steinbeck's house in Sag Harbor (New York) and found it. Steinbeck accosted them in his driveway and told them to beat it.

Yes, Deduck had been the professor.

I remember reading Ursula K. Leguin's *The Left Hand of Darkness*. Maybe Arthur C. Clarke's *Childhood's End*. And Frank Herbert's *Dune*—which has never left me. None of them have ever left me. But, mostly, I remember *The Handmaid's Tale*, by Margaret Atwood.

It wasn't my favorite, really. It still isn't.

It's embarrassing to admit, now, but I thought *Handmaid's Tale* was a little reactionary and maybe even paranoid. It was the 1980s and abortions were legal, people were prochoice.

Posthumous miniature portrait of Mary Shelley, who published *Frankenstein; or, The Modern Prometheus* (1818) at the age of twenty. The portrait was reportedly painted (after a death-mask) by Reginald Easton in 1857. *Public Domain.*[6]

And women were free to choose their partners and procreate or not. And have sex and abort the procreation process if they needed or wanted to. It was their body in the civilized world, and it seemed to me that people—even here in Texas—were mostly civil.

So, we read *The Handmaid's Tale* and went to discuss it in class. But we had a visitor.

Our custom was to sit in a circle as we discussed the assigned book, knowledge shared, ideas debated.

Our visitor was an attractive, somewhat older lady. Not showy, but sharp. Her hair was longer then, and dark brown. Professor Deduck introduced her.

It was Atwood. *Margaret Atwood.*

I don't remember what I said. She wasn't famous yet, but Atwood was the first serious writer I'd ever met face to face. I had a tendency to play contrarian (even then), but I don't think I did that day. I hope I didn't.

I doubt Atwood gave me a second thought. She was articulate and mildly daunting. But she wasn't arrogant or condescending. She answered our questions. My female classmates asked several. I was nonplussed.

I'd built up a tolerance. Cognitively speaking, my immune system was stronger by then. My early exposure had prepared me for deeper, prolonged exposures. I could be introduced to new ideas and different perspectives. I wasn't susceptible to most strains of close-mindedness. I could process new ideas, views, and opinions constructively, and allow them to challenge my weaker positions, my naivete, and even my own ignorance. I could also utilize them to fortify my better-informed perspectives, tweak them and articulate them more cogently. It happened more than once. It's still happening.

I was a carrier, and the more strains and contagions I was exposed to, the stronger I got.

Gabriel Garcia Marquez, Kurt Vonnegut. Alex Haley. Pablo Neruda.[7] Camille Paglia.[8] T.S. Elliott. Rainer Maria Rilke.[9] Anne Sexton. E.E. Cummings. Charles Bukowski. Sharon Olds (she also appeared at my university—I still have signed, dedicated copies of her work). John Gardner. Jack Kerouac. Emily Dickinson. Toni Morrison.

I didn't shelter in place or turn away from my own inadequacies. I exposed myself more and more.

All Quiet on the Western Front by Erich Maria Remarque. *Man's Search for Meaning* by Viktor Frankl. *The Last Picture Show* by Larry McMurtry. *The Razor's Edge* by W. Somerset Maugham. *The Unbearable Lightness of Being*, by Milan Kundera. *Things Fall Apart* by Chinua Achebe. *Goodbye to a River* by John Graves. Yukio Mishima. Che Guevara. Don DeLillo. *Confederacy of Dunces* by John Kennedy Toole. *My Ishmael* by Daniel Quinn. Hunter S. Thompson. Harold Pinter. Sam Shephard. Mark Medoff. Anthony Burgess. Dalton Trumbo. Randolph Bourne.

Frankenstein, again. *Heart of Darkness*, again. *Grapes of Wrath*, again. *Dune, My Ishmael*, again. "Bartleby, the Scrivener", *Billy Budd*, "The Lottery" by Shirley Jackson. "The Wager" by Anton Chekov. So many other contagions. So many additional infections, and, dissections. Inflections, really. Even vivisection.

Atwood had been prescient.

The Handmaid's Tale is practically Texas by decree, now.

McCullers saw it all at twenty-three. Real human beings, with open minds and daring hearts, are lonely hunters. Steinbeck got ahead of himself, or maybe just us. In the souls of the people the grapes of wrath may have been filling and growing heavy—growing heavy for the vintage—but they

"The Hunger Artist" and other Franza Kafka works had an indelible effect on me. *Wikipedia Commons*.[10]

were never harvested. We let them rot on the vine.

That's why we are where we are today.

I was a carrier for years, but my infection eventually spread. I am now a creator.

And here in Texas—where creators are the cure and more carriers are our only hope, an asinine, government-mandated inoculation to make Texans immune to intellectual development has become a commercial requirement—to preserve the status quo, ignorance—which is the most dangerous pandemic of them all.

There are fewer and fewer Margaret Atwoods every year, and less of the population is introduced to books like *The Handmaid's Tale*. The cable/streaming cough drop version is weak and less effective. The most constructive, evocative exposure is the book, the written word—the ineradicable imprint, the inimitable consumption of meaning—the most profound interaction with her mindfulness and her art.

Mary Shelley's husband Percy[11] was right. Poets are the unacknowledged legislators of the world. And that's why what they have to say is being mitigated on every social platform and censored in libraries. The spoon-fed, toddler gruel on iPhones or television is bland and contains less intellectual fiber.

As much as conservatives complained, raged, and protested about vaccinations and quarantines to protect against Covid 19, they love them, recommend them, and demand them to preserve statewide ignorance, imbecility and an odious lack of empathy.

And we all know why.

Empathy is an indirect form of telepathy.

A serious investigation can lead to mass germination.

An insightful anecdote *can be the antidote.*

The "Stoning of the Blasphemer" (1873). In Shirley Jackson's "The Lottery" (1948), "stoning" becomes a civic duty. *Public Domain*.

Conservatives consider conscientious, thoughtful creators anathema. Politicians want to limit the number of carriers and are committed to dumbing down members of their own constituencies to preserve general complacence.

It's despicable and dangerous. It's diabolical and dire. It spells our collective doom.

There is no plague like ignorance, and the Texas Legislature is mandating "vaccination" for us against the only remedy.

Texas for Breakfast

September 21, 2023

I know it's hard to fathom, but there really was a time when "Don't Mess with Texas" actually meant something, and not just in terms of litter.

It forewarned the uninitiated of bona fide bad-asses, legendary contrarians, daring dreamers, and serious politicians who had no qualms about taking fatuous pretenders out behind the proverbial woodshed and beating the living or figurative shite out of them.

Sam Houston once drubbed a U.S. congressman half to death with his cane in Washington, D.C.,[12] and practically walked away scot-free (His lawyer was Francis Scott Key![13]). Then, three decades later, during his second stint as governor of Texas, he jeered the Texas secession convention, refusing to swear loyalty to the Confederacy. A century later, Denison native Dwight D. Eisenhower, who served as the Supreme Commander of the Allied Forces during WWII and became a two-term U.S. president, would very bluntly throw staggering shade at the then-budding but insatiably greedy American Military Industrial Complex. JFK didn't heed Ike's remarks, and, though Lyndon Baines Johnson played along (to his discredit and, I think, regret), he also became the most progressive American president in history, enacting dozens of eye-popping rights, privileges, and freedoms that most Americans today take for granted. Then we traded longhorns for lambs, allowing our last real lion, Ann Richards (she had more brains and balls than Poppy or Sonny Boy Bush combined), to be ousted by Dubya's personal "turd blossom", Karl Rove.[14]

Since this act of nasty self-debasement, a gaggle of Republican oaf-keepers have spent the last three decades reducing our great state to what we are now—an international laughingstock.

Cattle manure. Openly deranged.

Semiautomatic rifle-packing asshats.

And this was well before the dog and Paxton pony fiasco.

We're no longer seen as a great state. We're viewed more like a backwards banana republic (emphasis on "banana"). Texas is now a joke, an adjectival term of derision, as in "those idiots went all Texas on us" or "that stupidity is Texas-level, yo!"

For educated Americans and most of the rest of the world, Texans are synonymous with shameless cretins, imbeciles, sexist morons, or chauvinist losers. The slow, Republican-led domestic intellectual plummet and resulting international perception shift have reduced us to a superficial, xenophobic, conformist dystopia. Which sincerely sucks, because we used to be the exception—not fascist fools.

Texas produced the first female sheriff, the first all-women state Supreme Court, the first woman on the U.S. Supreme Court (Sandra Day O'Connor), the first Black woman in the U.S. House of Representatives (Barbara Jordan[15]), and the first Chicano G.I. Joe (legendary Medal of Honor recipient Roy Benavidez). Texas was the home turf for the Civil Rights Act, the Voting Rights Act, the first Bilingual Education Act, *Roe*

Texas native Sandra Day O'Connor became the first female U.S. Supreme Court Justice on September 25, 1981. *Public domain.*

v. Wade, and dozens of landmarks that define the Great Society. Texas was even the base of operations for Madalyn Murray O'Hair and the American Atheists association and Mike Judge's *Beavis and Butthead* and *King of the Hill.*

Texas produced Janis Joplin, Stevie Ray Vaughan, Beyonce, Selena, Freddy Fender, Katherine Anne Porter,[16] Robert Rauschenberg, Erykah Badu, John Graves, Willie Nelson, Doug Sahm, the Butthole Surfers ... hell, even Black Panther Bobby Seale is a native Texan!

The Lone Star state also produced icons of the Third Estate, including Walter Cronkite, Molly Ivins, Dan Rather, and Jim Leher.

Today, Texas politics has descended into an ignorant crescendo of conformist, party-line blowhards like Greg Abbott, John Cornyn, and Ted Cruz. And Texas' national contributions to cultural and intellectual development rise to little more than lukewarm, rustic slop jars like Chip and Joanna Gaines, Jenna Bush Hager, Kelly Clarkson, Fort Worth Pascal High School's own Sheridan Taylor Gibler, Jr. (also known as Taylor Sheridan), and clueless, third-rate sophists like Alex Jones and Joe Rogan.

Lone Star icon Willie Nelson once said, "I'm from Texas, and one of the reasons I like Texas is because there's no one in control." And back when he said it, it was probably true. We used to be more open-minded. We were practical and believed in common sense. But Texas is no longer governed by pragmatism, assertive wit, or human decency. Texas has been reduced to a big, red, Republican Porta-Potty, where backwards wastrels launch excrement on the shithouse walls just to see what will stick under the graying, mustachioed upper lips of their, yes, deplorable constituencies and pass their hypocritical smell tests.

In 2021, the Texas Lege made abortions illegal and sexual assault rewarding, because raped women were no longer permitted to abort their vicious fecundators' offspring. On September 1, 2023, the Lege made it legal for God-bothering chaplains to serve as guidance counselors in public schools without certification or experience in classroom instruction—but, hey, they're at least qualified to explain to young female students how Mary was made preggers without her consent and how *groooooovy* that turned out!

And this immaculate transgression was followed by several other lapses into priggish asininity. The feckless Lege's new "death star" bill eliminates local civil ordinances around the state, including workplace protections and common-sense environmental regulations. Senate Bill 17 bans diversity and inclusion programs at public universities (because what's wrong with gubernatorial incumbents gathering boner mounts at places called "Niggerhead Ranch"?). Senate Bill 19 gives

Infowars far-right, alt-right radio personality and conspiracy theorist, Alex Jones. *Art by author.*

the checkless Lege the power to proclaim that only college instructors who obstruct diversity and inclusion can receive tenure. House Bill 900 gives the reckless Lege expanded parameters to ban books in Texas libraries — except the Bible, of course, the reading of which will soon be required by force and policed by the new armed hall monitors the Lege is encouraging to reduce the scourge of intellectual discourse.

Don't mess with Texas?

Heck, it's getting so that any half-conscious dunderhead with a pulse can eat Texas for breakfast. We're mindless buffoons walking around with Texas Lege-ratified "Kick Me" notes on our backs, wondering why everyone else is bent on making us butt-sore.

At one time, Texas may have been Willie's sublime free-for-all. Now, it's clearly not. One party has been running the show for too long, and its leaders and their rabid base refuse to think constructively, thrive on cultural impracticalities and historic inanity, and seem bent on making sure any semblance of conscience or enlightenment is fenced in.

Even some Aggies are appalled.

The slow, anti-intellectual deluge of Red State Kool-Aid has left Jim Bob Q. Public *Yellowstoned* (thanks, Gibler), and the party behind everything we used to rue seems to revel in seeing the rights of anyone who isn't straight, white, and a man's man male trod upon with impunity.

So *please* mess with Texas, friends.

Let's get rid of the real trash.

Lawrence M. Peters

November 20, 2023

His June 18, 1996 obituary in the *Fort Worth Star-Telegram* is short and succinct.

> *Lawrence M. Peters, 78, a retired Allied Mills employee, was found dead Friday* [June 13] *in Teague. Funeral: 11 a.m. today at Avant A.M.E. Church in Teague. Burial: Fairfield. Mr. Peters retired in 1982.*

It's not much of a lede, but it's where we should start.

Lawrence M. Peters died on June 13, 1996, and his obit ran on June 18. No picture. No next of kin listed. No mention of his loved ones.

Most of the obits around it have pictures of the deceased, several lines about the lives they led, and a list of survivors. Peters' is uninteresting.

It brings to mind an old English expression long claimed to be a Chinese curse: "May you live in interesting times." The adage is foreign to us, especially as social media trumpets the ways in which our lives are interesting, but in the old days, "interesting times" were often times of tribulation or danger.

Lawrence M. Peters' obit is boring but misleading. He lived in very interesting times.

A Fort Worth police officer inspects a bombed vehicle owned by a Lawrence M. Peters, a Black man who had just moved into white Riverside, in 1953. *Courtesy* Fort Worth Star-Telegram *archives.*

In the early 1950s, he worked as a bin stocker at Allied Mills on 401 N. Beach St. It's not clear where he lived before, but by 1953, he was thirty-five years old and making $55 a week. He and his wife had been saving for a while, and they had enough to finance a house. A decent house in the Riverside neighborhood just east of downtown Fort Worth. It was also just a five-minute drive to his job. He was living the American Dream, right here in Cowtown.

He paid $1,278 down on a two-bedroom frame home at 109 N. Judkins, and trouble began as soon as he unpacked on

August 21, 1953. Mr. and Mrs. Peters were Black. The Riverside neighborhood was white.

The "good" white citizenry of the neighborhood took immediate (though, perhaps in their minds, tactful) action. Upstanding white community leaders like George A. Seaman (a former city councilmember), Mack Dumas, Rayford M. Shelton, and George Brown formed the Riverside Merchants and Home Owners Association in response to the new residents. The association didn't want their nice, respectable suburbia encroached upon by "Negroes". Seaman and other association members met with Peters and offered to pay his down payment, plus equity and moving expenses, to leave.

"I want to stay," Peters told the *Fort Worth Star-Telegram*. "I worked hard and saved my money to buy a clean, decent home. I went to the real estate company to buy a house, and they sold me this one. I don't want any trouble with anyone. I wouldn't have moved in here if I'd had any idea it would upset these people, but now I've gone to the trouble of moving, and it's a nice home. I'd like to stay. I'll be a good citizen and a good neighbor."

On August 25, 1953, the real estate firm that sold the Peters couple their home announced it was canceling all future listings in the area "as a result of white protests over it and other companies offering homes for sale to Negroes."

But others slipped through.

On Saturday, September 26, an unidentified Black family tried to move into 113 N. Judkins—the house right next door to the Peters residence—and a belligerent crowd of white protesters was so unnerving and threatening that the incoming Black family loaded back up before they were even unpacked and left.

Before his Riverside house was bombed, a Black real estate agent had been warned by a number of white Riverside residents. *Courtesy* Fort Worth Star-Telegram *archives.*

When Peters returned home later, the white mob warned him, shouting that they "would put a bomb under" his car. Seaman later insisted that a number of folks "heckled the

Negroes moving into the house" next door but that no one had threatened Peters.

"Some of them just yelled at him that he had missed a party by coming home so late," Seaman said. "This is not a temporary deal. We're going to see this thing through, and we're going to win."

Seaman and the others planned meetings all over Riverside. "And by Riverside," Seaman clarified, "I mean Oakhurst, Haltom City, Oak Knoll, and Richland Hills."

The Riverside Merchants and Home Owners Association membership was limited to individuals who signed affidavits affirming that they were not Communists, that they would do "nothing to devaluate Riverside property", and that they were "Caucasians in race".

On Monday, August 31, the Fort Worth branch of the NAACP proposed the creation of a mayor-appointed biracial commission to promote a better understanding between whites and Blacks in the area. In an official statement, they issued constructive advice to all parties: "Look for qualities that are more than skin deep, and you will get excellent neighbors. If the people of Riverside and other areas in Fort Worth can begin judging neighbors on this democratic basis, we can contribute to the advance of human relations and serve as a model community in housing for other areas of these United States."

Soon, signs reading, "This house not for sale to Negroes" began greeting Peters from homes up and down his street. Then, during the wee hours of November 2, 1953, the empty residence at 113 N. Judkins was doused in gasoline and burned, and several sticks of dynamite were placed under the hood of Peters' car and detonated. The explosion blew out the front living room windows of the Peters house, and Peters was frustrated and defiant. When a reporter solicited his response

FBI Director J. Edgar Hoover gave Peters lip service over the phone, but didn't investigate. *Public domain*.

after the attack, he was bitterly unequivocal.

"Tell them I'm going to stay," Peters said. "Tell them I'm not going to move out."

After worrying for several hours that Monday, Peters contacted the FBI. After explaining his predicament to an aide of FBI Director J. Edgar Hoover, he spoke with Hoover himself. "I told him I needed protection because the police here didn't seem to be doing anything."

Hoover listened patiently and promised Peters he would send agents to Fort Worth to investigate. He never did. Mack Dumas from the Riverside Merchants and Home Owners Association suggested that the bombing may have been perpetrated by allies of the Negroes "to gain sympathy for their cause." Some suggested Peters had created a "Frankenstein" by moving to the Riverside area and that he couldn't leave 109 N. Judkins because he would be "letting other Negroes down."

Peters scoffed at the notion and stated that he was staying in the home for himself—"individually, not for other Negroes. I feel it's right. I bought the house with good intentions, and one of the intentions was to stay, so I'm going to."

On Tuesday, November 17, a second bomb detonated, shaking the home of L.V. Johnson, a Black 54-year-old real estate agent who had been handling house sales in the Riverside neighborhood for months. The blast, which was the result of dynamite placed near Johnson's front steps, occurred at 1:45 a.m. at 1514 Kennedy in a Black neighborhood near I.M. Terrell High School. The explosion chipped concrete, ripped siding, uprooted shrubbery, and shattered the windows of Johnson's property and a neighbor's. Johnson told WBAP-TV (now NBC 5) that he was just trying to "make a living."

Johnson, whose house was two miles away from the Peters residence, had been visited and warned by a number of white Riverside residents and was regularly receiving threatening phone calls. He bemoaned the unfair treatment.

"It's just a business with me," Johnson told the *Star-Telegram*. "I sell houses to a lot of people. This is my living, and I have to do it. It's true that some white people have listed

Whites bombed the car of a Black English teacher near Lake Como in 1954.
Courtesy Fort Worth Star-Telegram *archives*

their houses with me. All the white people came to me. I never went to them for the business."

The following day, the Fort Worth branch of the NAACP offered a $250 reward for any information that could help local authorities arrest and prosecute the individuals involved in the recent bombings in the area, but no one stepped forward.

For the next several months, white animosity in the Riverside community simmered steadily but revealed itself in more passive-aggressive ways. This changed on Saturday,

September 11, 1954, when dynamite was placed under the car of a Dunbar Junior High School English teacher named Kerven W. Carter, Jr. in front of his home at 5736 Diaz, near Lake Como. Carter, his wife, and their three-year-old son were awakened by the blast at 1:11 a.m., and the bombing method and pattern matched the earlier incidents involving Peters and Johnson.

Carter's parents had moved to 158 N. Judkins—situated between two white families—just nine days earlier, and Carter had been harassed when he visited them and then forced to contend with phone calls from people who wouldn't speak when he or his wife answered.

Seaman was surprised, though he noted that even though the number of Black residents in the Riverside area was growing, the Riverside Merchants and Home Owners Association hadn't had a meeting in months.

"This is a bad thing," Seaman told the *Star-Telegram*. "What this city needs is for a Negro to move into TCU, Ridglea, Westcliff, or Westover Hills. Then they would see what our problem is out here."

The bombing destroyed Carter's two-year-old vehicle and blew out some of the windows in his house.

According to a report by the City of Fort Worth titled "Historic Context of Fort Worth: Postwar Suburbanization and Development, 1946-1980", a "shifting demographic played out in neighborhoods, including Morningside, Van Zandt, Terrell Heights, and Riverside, where Black families moved, as well as in Diamond Hill, where Latino families relocated. The integration prompted some white families to leave these neighborhoods and move to new, outlying, predominantly white suburbs. Other white families remained, and in some cases the integration resulted in racial tensions and violence. In Van Zandt and Morningside, white residents staged demonstrations, and at least one dynamite bomb was placed on the porch of a Black-owned house. The worst case of racial violence, though, occurred in Riverside, where protests, house burnings, and bombings occurred for several years in the late 1950s."

A WBAP news report from September 2, 1956, illustrates this point. It begins with images of a flyer announcing a meeting at the Riverside Elementary School "in the interest of preserving your community, your home, and separate schools for your children" and saying that a "Negro [is] moving in at 209 N. Judkins." The wording at the bottom of the flyer indicates it was created by the Riverside Merchants and Home Owners Association. The clip then features images of E.G. Brown speaking to white citizens, calling for action against a Black man named Lloyd Austin and his family, who are the new residents of 209 N. Judkins. About 200 whites—men, women, and children—attend the meeting and plan a protest march in front of the Austin family's new residence. The clip then introduces Diamond Hill resident Jack Lamont and records him admitting he's "for hanging Negroes" as he prepares signs for the protest. Next up is Seaman, who recommends that economic pressure be applied at Lloyd Austin's and his wife's places of employment to get them fired.

The next bit of footage chronicles the white crowd leaving Riverside Elementary School with their signs and heading for 209 N. Judkins. The white mob is transported by automobiles and soon floods the street and sidewalks of the 200 block of N. Judkins with defiant white faces and their signs. One says, "Nigger Get Out." Another says "Better STAY OUT NIG and stay alive." Fellow Black residents along the street, including

Peters, join Lloyd Austin in his house. Police arrive and monitor the situation but eventually depart.

Near dark, a group of approximately forty white boys gather in front of the Austin home and hurl rocks and soda bottles at it. Fifty other white residents stand and simply watch. Several windows in the Austin home are shattered, but the police are no longer around.

Then shots are fired.

The next footage shows a crowd surrounding a car parked in front of the Austin residence. The camera captures bullet holes in the hood and the radiator of the vehicle.

Later, the white youths display an effigy they had reportedly hanged in a nearby tree. They say a "Negro" man cut it down. The Fort Worth police return and begin dispersing the white crowd and send the boys home.

The seventieth anniversary of the beginning of this reign of domestic terror in Fort Worth was November 2, 2023. Very few people in Fort Worth remember or acknowledge it, and any books or textbooks that might discuss the incident and others that followed would probably not be allowed on the shelves of Fort Worth schools or libraries—but Lawrence M. Peters refused to give up his seat on the proverbial bus two years before Rosa Parks.[17] And he stood up before Martin Luther King Jr. and Malcolm X right here in Fort Worth, and none of us have ever heard of him. "Lawrence M. Peters" is just 30 dispassionate words in a forgotten 1996 obit.

We all know the drill. What's done is done, and it was done by somebody else to somebody else. And it's still being done today to somebody else.

Even though we live in interesting times, we clearly don't care. Our chief preoccupation is selective disinterest.

Seven Generations Behind

August 31, 2023

It's funny. You think you know a place. A community.

Maybe it's the town you grew up in. Maybe it's a city you've lived in for decades. Perhaps it's a state or even a country.

Your primary and secondary schools gave you comic book versions of the place's history and heroes, and then you were on your merry way. You did the normal things, pursued the typical ends, and enjoyed standard success. You assumed a life.

But somewhere along the way, you remembered something off-putting at a red light or recalled a disturbing image you saw on TV. A face in a crowd or a voice in the back of your head. It unsettled you. Something rattled the acquiescence you had eased into and the cozy assimilation you eventually wore like a letter jacket for adulthood.

Something undermined it and, with it, you.

Most people's attention to this kind of existential glitch drifts when the TV channel changes or the red light turns green, and they may never revisit it again. Why should they? It was an exception, not the rule. They have their children's college fund

"Yes, and he who thinks, what's more, he who makes thought his business, he may go far in it, but he has bartered the solid earth for the water all the same, and one day he will drown." –Herman Hesse, *Steppenwolf*.

to save for and retirement. They shush the stray notions away or shove them out of the foreground.

Few of them have read Herman Hesse,[18] but a short passage from *Steppenwolf* perfectly illustrates their stance on the matter. People won't swim, Hesse suggests. "They are born for the solid earth, not for the water. And naturally they won't think. They are made for life, not for thought. Yes, and he who thinks, what's more, he who makes thought his business, he may go far in it, but he has bartered the solid earth for the water all the same, and one day he will drown."

It's a fair point. Who wants to drown?

Can you name a single person from wherever you grew up who was really interested in swimming? Didn't almost all of them prefer the safety of solid ground?

Dylan Thomas[19] was a fine swimmer, but he knew there was no future in his "craft or sullen art" and that he'd be treading water 'til the end. Anne Sexton[20] approached the issue more practically.

"Live or die," she wrote, "but don't poison everything."

Hesse and Thomas were the types of friends you let drift away. Sexton killed herself.

Yes.

To think is to undermine. And sinking is the danger of thinking, so we desperately cling to false buoyancies like capitalism, religion, or technology. We know they're nothing more than garbage patches spinning in the ocean, but a temporary respite from our anxieties is better than nothing.

So here we are. We find ourselves in a time and a place where the complacence that was once guaranteed by standard, obligatory distractions and gaieties is failing us. And we seem to have forgotten how to swim.

Existential urgency encroaches from every direction, including rising, poisoned seas, but only a teenage girl from Sweden has taken to the water.

Does this make us pathetic or simply apathetic?

Our leaders use one to reinforce the other. They certainly work real hard to keep us from abandoning solid ground.

Serious thought processes are what the times require, and I thought my home state and my country were full of serious people. We certainly need to be. We're seven generations behind.

The average period constituting one generation to the next is twenty to thirty years, and seven generations back, the first Industrial Revolution was about to be supplanted by the second. Meanwhile, our efforts to extinguish or convert our indigenous neighbors—many of whom believed that every major decision in their tribe should be made keeping the well-

Greta Thunberg[21] in Stockholm (2023). *Wikipedia Commons*.

being of the seventh generation forward in mind—were really picking up steam. It was happening to indigenous and aboriginal peoples all over the world, and the white refrain was always the same. The indigenous or aboriginal peoples were considered godless, primitive savages, uneducated, uncivilized, and, in many cases, subhuman.

Boy, do we have egg on our face now.

The Great White Lie that our ways were better than theirs is finally and indisputably being exposed. We don't even think one generation ahead, much less seven—and our stewardship of the planet and the human population that inhabits it has been cataclysmic and may be unsalvageable.

The white guys were never the smartest folks in the room. Just the greediest and the ones who paid the least heed to living in harmony with their environment and the world around them. Their air. Their water sources. And their animal kin.

Ultimately—and probably until the end—we are the worst lice in creation, and every conscious, sentient creature that isn't us knows it.

But we're on solid ground.

And they'll all drown.

Rally Crowd Full of Ignorance, Insanity

I went to the anti-war rally on Wednesday. I would like to tell you what I saw, what I heard. Let me tell you first that I left the event shaking, unable to speak, wanting only to lash out.

I wanted to crush skulls, smash them to pieces, burn them to ash, grind them to powder, reduce them to nothingness. I wanted to crack misshapen conches and let the spoiled, unused, worthless contents seep out onto the concrete.

I don't consider myself a violent person.

I am simply prone to fierce, violent reactions to ignorance. Insanity often has that effect on the sane.

The crowd contained a healthy brood of ignorance and its cohorts: fear and macho inanity. Men in camouflage pants—high on testosterone and propaganda—turned red, white and blue—shouting imbecilic rebukes accordingly. Men in cowboy hats, mostly dim yokels, agreed and offered personal insults, as if to accent their case. Fraternity men nodded approvingly, and occasionally offered justifications for an invasion for economic reasons. It was typical.

"Leave the country," these men yelled at the peace-pushers.

Quasi-Texan comedian and satirist Bill Hicks knew Operation Desert Storm was a charade and constantly wrankled American rubes. "There never was a war," he said. "A war is when *two* armies are fighting." The punchline: during the Gulf War there were 147 U.S. casualties and at least 22,000 Iraqi casualties. *Wikipedia Commons.*[22]

"You wanna pay ten bucks for a gallon of gas," these men shouted at the peace-freaks. "Communist pigs," these men screamed at the life-lovers. "Have you ever had heterosexual sex," one man roared, delighted with his logic.

These men went on, so secure, so sure in their advocation of bloodshed. So passionate about war and killing. So sure about their murderous intent. I wondered if they realized that the same mentality crucified their savior. I wondered how secure and satisfied they would be with bayonets through their hearts, their bodies twisting writhing, dying in some rat-infested pile of spent puppets. I supposed they could find some solace in their God.

He's a warmonger, too.

These heroes, these patriots; they went on and on. They asked some of the protesters if they would "serve their country" if they were called upon. The protesters' answer was negative. The heroes and patriots called them traitors and cowards. These "real" Americans provided a compelling display of something really American: ignorance.

I made a decision at that rally.

Disgusted with my people and ashamed of my country, I came to a conclusion. My revelation is a sad one. I am not comfortable with it, but it is my heart.

I will not fight in the sands of Iraq. I will not fight on Russian soil. I refuse to denounce Fidel Castro. I refuse to support the Contras in Nicaragua. I refuse to take up arms in any Third World country I can think of, because we have oppressed them and worked hard to deny them even the most basic human rights at every turn. If they conquered us tomorrow, we'd deserve it.

I refuse to fight against practically every faction my government says is in the wrong, because the American government is too often in the wrong and its motives are profit-oriented, not moral or ethics or even people-oriented. I may fight someday, but probably not on my government's side. For instance, I would fight against the white regime we support in South Africa; I would fight with the Palestinians against Israel; I would fight against any of the number of puppet dictatorships we've installed in South and Central America. And, are you ready for the kicker?

I would fight in a civil war in this country.

If intellect and ignorance squared off tomorrow, I would take up arms. I would smash and crack and destroy every stupid head I could reach, and I would die like a dog. My body would be mutilated and burned because conscience would lose miserably in this country.

Hate, fear, greed, prejudice, insanity and ignorance outnumber it a thousand to one.

Travel Ban

August 8, 2023

I like travelling. I did a lot of it when I was younger, especially international. I didn't get to visit as many places as I'd like, but I was able to see a fair share. I liked to see and experience things.

Into my thirties, a beautiful woman took me to be her lawful, wedded husband, and we started a family. I traveled less overseas and more around Texas. I was able to see new parts of my home state with my family and experience varied and fascinating places and things with my wife and kids.

In the early aughts, I began dabbling in freelance journalism, doing some writing about the fun-filled, profound travel experiences I'd had with my kids. In fact, one of the first pieces I had published in a major Texas magazine detailed something we'd discovered together on one of our excursions.

Later on, I was approached by the Reedy Press to write a travel guide about a city in Texas. I told them I wasn't interested in writing a travel book about a particular community, but I would be interested in tackling the entire state.

The Reedy Press said they didn't do "statewide" travel guides, so I politely declined their offer and thanked them for their interest. Then they got back with me, agreeing to publish a statewide travel guide. I was thrilled. The first edition of *100 Things to Do in Texas Before You Die* was published in 2018, to no small acclaim. It included some images of my kids and discussions related to experiences I'd had with my wife and children. It was the chronicle of the fulfillment of a dream.

You see, early on, I'd begun carrying colored markers and 4-by-6 index cards along with us on our journeys, and after experiencing some adventures or taking in some of the sights, I encouraged my kids to draw pictures of what they'd seen or experienced on the blank side of the index cards. Then we converted them into postcards, scribbling a blurb and our address on the opposite side and placing a stamp. I had postcard records of some of the experiences and a treasure trove of memories in a stack of index cards held together by a rubber band. Family fun as a secret weapon when I went to write the book.

100 Things to Do in Texas Before You Die was well-received and a success for Reedy Press. In fact, within a year or three, they'd published six or seven other "state" travel guides and one on Puerto Rico!

In early 2022, Reedy approached me to do a second edition of my Texas travel guide, and I initially balked. I had too much going on. I didn't know what else I had to add. But then I reread the first edition. I realized I'd missed a few things and, occasionally, been a little high hat. I'd neglected subjects like NASCAR and professional wrestling, which, though not appealing to me, did appeal to many Texans and comprised phenomena that Texas played a huge part in the history of.

I agreed to do a second edition, and it was released on October 13, 2022—the birthday of my oldest twin children. It was thrilling, again, and something I was very proud of. To borrow a phrase from legendary, recently departed Czech-

My 6-year-old daughter's depiction of fishing with her younger brother or one of our dogs at South Llano River State Park (2004).

French Nobel Laureate Milan Kundera, the "unbearable lightness of being" (and/or wonderful, sustaining memories of real-life excitement and adventures) never really leaves you, and it's a joy to share it—especially twice. And especially when it depicts the thrill of exploring the richness, diversity, and numerous wonders of the state of Texas!

The thing is, however, the Reedy Press stipulated that I do a certain number of events and appearances to promote the book, so several months back, I lined up something local. Right here in Fort Worth. I arranged to do a reading, signing, and Q&A at the Ridglea Public Library on September 21, 2023. I set up the appearance and marked it on the calendar. I was elated. Maybe even some of my kids, now grown, could be there.

In the meanwhile, I noticed that the files I'd accumulated for over a dozen nonfiction books I'd written (on heavier subjects) and historical markers I'd worked on now practically filled an entire closet. The material was near and dear to me, but there were reams of information and files chock-full of subjects I'd never get around to writing about.

I needed to store it elsewhere. And I needed to store it somewhere that other researchers might have access to it.

I contacted the Mary Couts Burnett Library at TCU.

It permitted local access for me, afforded my papers the prestige of one of the most respected Lone Star State universities, and it was an institution my parents always loved. I had been a Texas State University grad, but I still had a soft spot for the Horned Frogs, and I knew plenty of talented folks who had attended TCU.

The library personnel seemed excited about the acquisition of my research, and I donated the lot. In fact, I handed it over for cataloging on August 1, 2023. All it required was the signing of a three-page agreement, granting them the copyrights to my nonfiction research. It could be stored there for posterity. It could be housed there to spur future historical investigations and scholarly works. This, too, was thrilling.

On Friday, July 21, however, I had gotten an email from the Fort Worth Public Library folks informing me that I'd receive a second email with a contract that I'd have to sign to secure the stamp of officialdom that sanctioned my appearance to discuss travel in Texas on September 21.

I got busy with other things and didn't even open it.
Five days later, I got a second email reminding me that I needed to open the contract, give it my electrical "John Hancock," and return it, so the next day, I opened it.

The first thing that struck me was the length of the document. It ran eleven pages.

Sheesh, I thought. That's longer than my introductory presentation on Texas travel at the event would be. I was more a fan of the Q&A, swapping pointers, sharing adventures, and hearing recommendations of different places in Texas to give a gander.

The document also had to be accessed in Adobe Acrobat Sign, and though I wanted to read a hard copy, I couldn't figure out how to print it, so I started plodding through the droll onscreen scroll. There were over thirty sections and some of the last few stopped me in my tracks.

I was identified—contractually, by the document—as a "performer." OK, I thought. But, as a performer, some of the last few sections were clearly unconstitutional and blatantly mandated censorship. They didn't have anything to do with what I wanted to talk about at the Ridglea Library and they were an insult to my rights as a Texan and an American.

I could hardly believe my eyes.

There were stipulations tucked into the contract that didn't

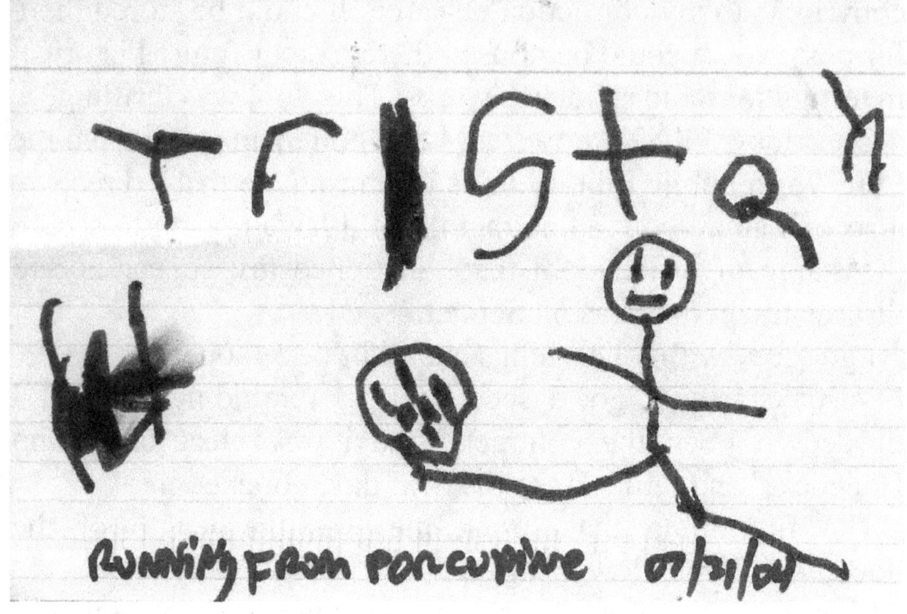

My 5-year-old son's rendering of fleeing from a porcupine at South Llano River State Park (2004).

seem very Texan at all. I recorded some of the despotic vernacular and shook my head.

To wit, if I wanted to go extol the virtues of traveling and really seeing Texas (swapping pointers, detailing wondrous road trips, and sharing my enthusiasm for exploring my Lone Star home) at a Fort Worth public library, I had to commit to various (and arguably nefarious) Texas government codes and acts:

> Section "**XXX. PROHIBITION OF BOYCOTTING ENERGY COMPANIES**" stipulated that as said "Performer," (1) I do not "boycott energy companies; and (2) will not boycott energy companies during the term of this agreement."

Hell, No. 60 in *100 Things to Do in Texas Before You Die* is "Explore Gushers at the East Texas Oil Museum" in Kilgore.

Section "**XXXI. PROHIBITION ON DISCRIMINATION AGAINST FIREARMS AND AMUNITIONS INDUSTRIES**" stipulated that the "Performer's signature provides written verification to City that Performer: (1) does not have a practice, policy, guidance, or directive that discriminates against a firearm entity or firearm trade association; and (2) will not discriminate against a firearm entity or firearm trade association during the term of this agreement."

Number 58 in *100 Things to Do in Texas Before You Die* is "Trace the Footsteps of Doc Holiday and Wyatt Earp at Fort Griffin" in Albany.

Oh, and somewhere prior to these sections the contract stipulated that I can't boycott (i.e., badmouth) Israel.

This was not thrilling.

It was chilling.

Does the Texas state legislature harbor a gaggle of retired Kremlin, KGB, or old Stasi[23] castoffs to write policy for it now? Is this what a Texas travel advocate has to sign to share travel tips, off-the-beaten-path tidbits, or tales of epic meanderings?

Is this who we are now?

Is this what Texans really believe in?

Has Texas become a fascist state?

I subsequently replied to the contractee, informing them that I could not in good conscience sign the contract. Selling a few books about Texas travel is a good thing—but, sorry, not at the risk of selling your soul as a Texan.

Real Atlases

January 6, 2022

The other early evening, I was standing in the front entry near the register at one of my favorite local eateries. I was by myself and waiting for a table. The diners were still spaced according to COVID protocol, and the thirtysomething female proprietor was discussing a reservation with a spry septuagenarian woman.

The female elder had pulled in before me and parked right in front of the front door. Her car was something nice, expensive and European. The eatery lay in close proximity to Westover Hills, and I was standing in close proximity to the proprietor and the septuagenarian's conversation.

The elder needed a reservation for eight on such and such day, and the proprietor was politely explaining to her that tables on that date were not available. The elder stressed the imperative nature of the date and the reservation, and the proprietor politely explained and re-explained that a table on said date was unfortunately impossible. The conversation went on for quite a while, and I was impressed with the proprietor's patience and civility.

The elder—who noted that she was a frequent customer— was agitated, but the proprietor remained courteously clear. The eatery was down to one chef, one waitperson, and the proprietor was picking up the slack. Like many businesses around Cowtown, the place was struggling to find help, and the employees who were showing up were overworked, overstressed, and doing the best they could. At one point, the proprietor even asked the elder if she had any high school or college age grandchildren or grandnephews/nieces who needed a job. The labor shortage was stark and prolonged, and, again, the eatery was doing the best it could with the staff it had.

The elder was not confused or bewildered—she simply didn't care. She reemphasized that she'd been a customer there for years. I almost laughed out loud when she then said, "Can't you just push two tables together?"

The extraordinarily patient proprietor kept her cool but kindly explained, "I'm sorry, but that would hardly help. The tables on that date already have people sitting at them."

The conversation was becoming a small spectacle, and I was getting hungry. But I was wildly impressed with the proprietor's unflinching professionalism, and I thought the matter had reached its conclusion. I was wrong.

The elder fumed, harrumphed, and started to turn and then turned back and demanded to see the proprietor's "books."

"I beg your pardon," the proprietor replied.

By "books," I could only assume the elder meant the proprietor's reservation log, but still. It was like a Gestapo[24] command.

The proprietor held her ground, and, after a long moment, the elder eventually departed. I didn't get the impression the elder was in any way pacified or sympathetic. In fact, when she turned to leave, I got the impression that her passing glare assigned me to the same class as the uncooperative proprietor.

Servant.

Peasant.

Little people.

The proprietor apologized to me for the wait and the small spectacle, and I told her I was knocked out by her extraordinary composure and self-restraint. But I had to know—was the frustrated elder even a good tipper?

"No," the proprietor smiled. "She was one of the worst."

Now, I'm not exactly in the business of criticizing cheapskates or my elders, and, to be fair, this isn't a problem stemming from age or frugality. Post-COVID—or quasi-post-COVID—America is radically different and probably not just temporarily. In the good ol' days and right up to COVID protocols, most of us spent much more time making a living than doing much living—or thinking about how we were living our lives. COVID shutdowns and the subsequent COVID relief checks gave us more time to reflect. We eventually experienced Netflix burnout and boredom and lingering discontent. American culture had molded us to be happy little consumers with materialistic perspectives, but our wages and salaries were purchasing us less and less and Fortune 500 CEOs were *taking* more and more. And obscenely wealthy billionaires were conducting field trips to space with Captain Kirk. The closest the working class came to really living or going to space or experiencing adventure were the multi-season period dramas on streaming platforms.

And then it happened.

A large swathe of the overworked, underappreciated, and under-compensated working public realized that Ramen noodles weren't that bad, especially if eating out a lot required reducing themselves to the wage-slavery that our tax-dodging so-called job creators offered us.

Why not get by on less and be content with less? Why not lounge around on the dole? Why not freelance? *Why even bother having kids, especially if what they'll have to deal with is the same servitude that most of us were born into?*

Our political leadership steps to the tune of billionaires and brainwashed boomers—and their futures are already assured. Meanwhile, the working class is facing increasingly pension-less grinds, poverty-level minimum wages, and rising food and housing costs. Futures without real promise. Futures with very little hope.

The Great Resignation is a serious problem, but it's been a long time coming. Ayn Rand and Paul Ryan and Rand Paul (and legions of their pseudointellectual ilk) have always gotten it wrong. People like Elon Musk, Jeff Bezos, and the Koch brothers were never Atlases. They were always the load the working public lifted up. And the billionaire class continues to grow exponentially, insanely, and, again, obscenely wealthy, while the real Atlases' futures and existential prospects grow dim. So, a daunting cross-section of the working class is shrugging.

Mightily.

No Country for Old Racists

February 8, 2023

Today, a mixed bag. Good news and bad news.

Remember the main coin flip scene in *No Country for Old Men*, which is set in Texas? It now resonates in a whole new way.

For the uninitiated, stoic assassin Anton Chigurh (Javier Bardem) walks into a backcountry West Texas convenience store, and, after what he clearly perceives to be an absurd encounter with the rustic, elderly store proprietor, decides the universe might be better off without said proprietor. Chigurh is a nihilistic figure who claims no proprietary leanings in in terms of judging good or bad or right or wrong, necessarily—he just considers the elderly man's tired, down-home witticism and sedimentary resignation an affront to the living. I guess it's good he isn't God.

Chigurh does, however, entertain sporting chances.

"What's the most you ever lost on a coin toss?" he asks the man.

"I don't know," the proprietor says. "I couldn't say."

Chigurh flips a quarter, catches it, and places it on the wooden checkout counter surface, covering it with three fingers.

"Call it," he says.

The proprietor eyes him unsurely. "Call it?"

"Yes."

"For what?" the proprietor says.

"Just call it."

There is a long pause, the elderly man's mind slowly sifting through the possible implications of this strange wager. "Well, we need to know what we're calling it for, here."

Chigurh is mildly vexed. "You need to call it. I can't call it for you. It wouldn't be fair."

The proprietor thinks for a moment. "I didn't put nothing up."

Chigurh face flashes almost reptilian. "Yes, you did. You've been putting it up your whole life . . . You just didn't know it."

The elderly man flails, motionlessly and nonverbally.

"Do you know what date is on this coin?" Chigurh says.

"No."

"Nineteen-fifty-eight. It's been traveling for 22 years to get here. Now, it's here, and it's either heads or tails, and you have to say or call it."

"Well, look, I need to know what I stand to win."

"Everything," Chigurh replies chillingly.

"How's that?"

Chigurh is annoyed but never out of control.

"You stand to win everything," he pronounces.

There is another pause.

"Alright," the proprietor says. "Heads, then."

Chigurh slowly reveals the coin under his fingers. It's heads.

"Well done," he says.

Image by author.

The attendant begins to scoop up the coin and put it in his pocket, but Chigurh takes exception.

"Don't put it in your pocket," he says, his visage almost friendly.

"Sir?" the proprietor musters.

"Don't put it in your pocket. It's your lucky quarter."

"Where do you want me to put it?" the proprietor says.

"Anywhere," Chigurh advises, "but not in your pocket, where it will get mixed in with the others and become just a coin," Chigurh acknowledging the irony, "which it is."

And he leaves.

It's a Kafkaesque scene with sprinkles of Vonnegut and David Lynch, but it gets worse or better—or at least more interesting—today.

A 1958 quarter featured George Washington's profile (facing left) on the front, and, on the back, a bald eagle clutching an olive branch. George Washington, our first head of state, obviously signified heads. The bald eagle, our national bird, was tails.

Now, however, George's profile can be facing right or left on one side, and the back no longer features a bald eagle. It can be a state or a national park. It can be another important American historical figure and usually a historically underrepresented figure. I think it's exciting news, a coinage version of a 1980s box of Crackerjacks or Forrest Gump's box of chocolates in the 1990s.

You really don't know what you're going to get, and this amuses me (and perhaps you).

But it won't amuse some.

This is, after all, Black History Month, and I hate to vex Lone Star conservatives, but the quarters you pocket today often feature two heads and, arguably, no real tails. Why, a new shiny quarter I examined the other day had Frederick Douglass on it. A Black man on our legal tender?! Another new quarter I unknowingly pocketed to join my Critical Race Theory-applied coinage featured Maya Angelou[25] opposite George Washington. Two heads! One featuring an old white guy who, yes, was our first president but owned slaves (an institution the descendants of the beneficiaries of now discuss with their tails between their legs), the other featuring a towering Black female poet and civil rights activist whose voice and vision were commanding.

So which side now signifies tails?

I keep these lucky quarters, which also feature Wilma Mankiller (first woman elected principal chief of the Cherokee Nation), Anna May Wong (first Chinese American film star in Hollywood), Dr. Sally Ride (physicist, astronaut, educator, and first American woman in space), and Nina Otero-Warren (a leader in New Mexico's suffrage movement and the first female superintendent of Santa Fe public schools), plus this year two native Texans—Jovita Idar (Mexican-American journalist, activist, teacher, and suffragist) and Bessie Coleman (first African American and first Native American woman pilot)—will appear. As I giddily revel in these small steps in American evolution, I would argue that they are just as important today as our original revolution was.

Our Empire Strikes Back

August 17, 2022

One thing I think most bipedal, opposable-thumbed, prefrontal-cortexed mammals of the human variety can agree on: COVID sucks. And, after COVID, someone left the microwave going outside, and people are starting to wear masks again. Contractor, detractor, overreactor, denier, or decrier of the COVID-19 virus, surely none of us want to see it come back, especially writ large and in charge.

But what if you aren't a bipedal, opposable-thumbed mammal with a prefrontal lobe?

Coronavirus lockdowns were almost insufferable for us, but it was an invigorating refresher for Mother Nature, a year and a half at a health spa—and the first "spring break" that the rest of the species we share this wheezing blue orb with enjoyed in a half century.

The natural Bosphorus Strait, an internationally significant waterway in northwestern Turkey, hadn't seen many dolphins in decades. Part of the continental boundary between Asia and Europe, it was always too jammed with tankers, cargo ships and passenger boats, and—though we like to ignore it—

President John F. Kennedy presents the National Geographic Society's Gold Medal to pioneering oceanographer, writer and underwater filmmaker, Jacques Cousteau on April 19, 1961. Cousteau had stark opinions on overpopulation. *Public domain*.

dolphins are no dummies. An amphibious mammal, Mr. Dolphin also has a prefrontal cortex, and he doesn't play Roadrunner or Wile E. Coyote around major human traffic routes. But then Coronavirus appeared like the brave 5th-Century B.C. Roman general Coriolanus[26] and drove Madame and Monsieur Dolphins' nihilistic, suicidal human cousins back, and the amphibious mammals' kindred were seen swimming and frolicking up and down the Bosphorus.

In Albania, pink flamingos made a comeback on the country's western coastline. In Israel, wild boars roamed the streets freely. In Thailand, a wondrous, declining population of dugongs (a pudgy English bulldog-looking cousin of the manatee) held forth along the coastline and around the islands of Hat Choi Mai National Park after Coriolanus—*uhhh*, Coronavirus, I meant to say—cleared a tourist-swollen aneurysm and created a decline in water pollution. Wild cougars began appearing in the streets of Santiago, Chile; peacocks strutted around the square in Ronda, Spain; and the near-mythical Kashmiri goats of Wales descended from the Great Orme headlands and took over the deserted village of Llandudno.

In my own west Tarrant County neighborhood, I saw more deer, wild turkeys, turtles, and coyotes than ever before. Coriolanus—sorry, Coronavirus—kept bipedal, opposable-thumbed, prefrontal-cortexed mammals of the human variety indoors and granted the rest of the animal kingdom a breather. And the planet's atmosphere as well.

But now, in *Star Wars* terms, the "Empire" is striking back. And in *Stranger Things* vernacular, the human legion we know as the "Demogorgon" has returned. The most dangerous creature in our world has slipped free of its containment, and we're now a threat to innocent, metaphorically natural high school geeks and Metallica guitar solos everywhere. Humanity is "Darth Vader," and lovable dolphins, dugongs, Welsh fairy goats, Spanish peacocks, and pink flamingos are taking cover or running for their abbreviated lives, maybe for the rest of those lives.

If it wasn't so existentially irresponsible, sickening, and sad, it would seem silly. A few generations back, no one would have believed it possible. And yet here we are, with our fingers on the buttons, triggers, and lethal injection syringes that determine the fate of almost every other species on the planet, who, it should be mentioned, do not enjoy pension or retirement plans.

It makes me think about something that Jacques Cousteau,[27] the controversial but perhaps greatest and certainly one of the most outspoken conservationists in human history, said thirty years ago.

> *Getting rid of viruses is an admirable idea, but it raises enormous problems. In the first 1,400 years of the Christian era, population numbers were virtually stationary. Through epidemics, nature compensated for excess births by excess deaths . . . What should we do to eliminate suffering and disease? It's a wonderful idea but perhaps not altogether a beneficial one in the long run. If we try to implement it, we may jeopardize the future of our species . . . Mankind has probably done more damage to the Earth in the 20th century than in all of previous human history . . . It's terrible to have to say this. The world population must be stabilized, and to do that, we must eliminate 350,000 people per day. This is so horrible to contemplate that we shouldn't even say it. But the general situation in which we are involved is lamentable.*

The World Population Clock is just tics away from eight billion[28] and, here in Texas, we're arguing about birth control.

Tens of thousands if not hundreds of thousands of every living thing that isn't human are becoming endangered or

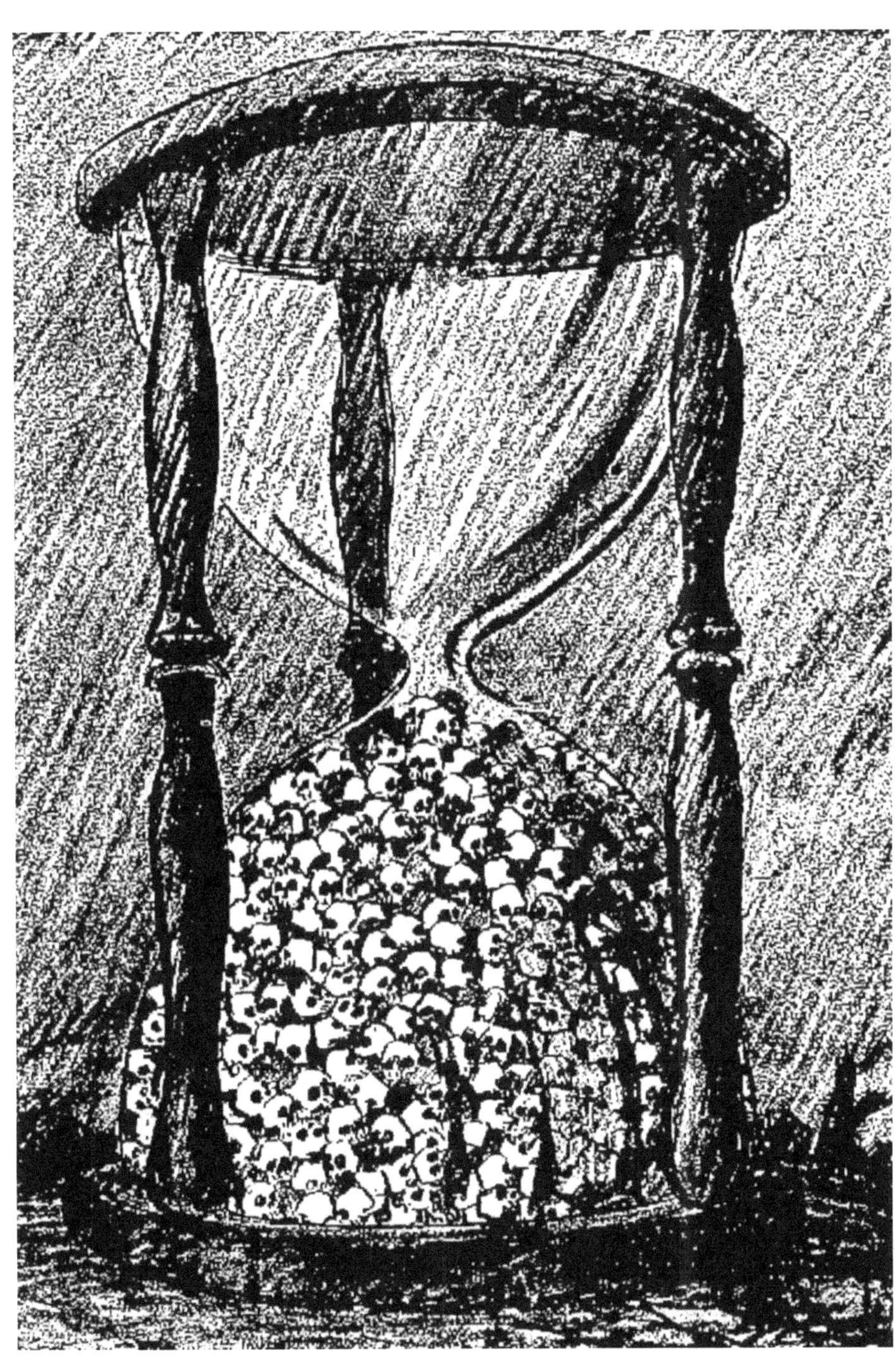

Brownsville Herald, July 26, 1937.[29]

going extinct every year and whole ecosystems that support these besieged innocents are about to collapse or simply vanish.

To paraphrase a line from another pop-culture mainstay, do we have any control over how creepy we'll allow ourselves to get? Because if this is *As Good as It Gets*,[30] and we're as good as we're going to get, the coronavirus pandemic was a promising moment, and now the majority of our fish, fowl, mammal, insect, and otherwise animate planetary cohabitants are completely fucked.

Dare I issue a call for Coriolani?

Do we have to perish to make the world livable again?

Shoulders of Goliath

January 19, 2022

On Veterans Day, it's typical and appropriate to see countless homages, salutes, and earnest formal and informal appreciation ceremonies for military servicemen and servicewomen in every electronic and paper medium that we encounter. It's part of who we are. It's part of how we got where we are.

I get it. We all get it.

Sometimes, however, Veterans Day observances annoy me. And not because I'm unpatriotic. I simply feel conflicted.

I've been told—or, perhaps, better put, "corrected"—that America is not the land of the free, home of the brave, but, in fact, the land of the free because of the brave.

Is this really true?

I don't think most folks would find my answer or my questions very patriotic.

Last January 16 marked the 30th anniversary of the six-week Gulf War in Iraq. This past September marked the 20th anniversary of 9/11, which resulted in the invasion of Iraq (again, in 2003), which had nothing to do with the 9/11 attack, so let's be honest. Back then, were the national pep rallies and resultant increased military enlistments to wage these wars a

American soldier in Da Nang, South Vietnam, 1967. *Public Domain.*

product of bravery *or military-industrial complex knavery? Or simple dupery?*

Former vice president—and Halliburton magnate—Dick Cheney[31] is smiling.

Should I defend my country, right or wrong? Seems like that's a painful mistake we've made in the past.

Should I simply love it or leave it?

Philosophically speaking, the infamous, pro-war "Love It or Leave" charge is a classic false dilemma. It reduces an issue to a puerile, simplistic either/or proposition. Americans really seem to love simplistic either/or propositions, but they're hardly ever useful or productive—or correct.

World War II can be viewed as a legitimate, necessary either/or equation that we, in the end—or 'til the end—needed to answer and did answer. And arguably well. Except in the end. The use of nuclear weapons on unsuspecting civilian population centers was arguably the greatest single-instant terrorist act in human history.

The Korean War was hardly legitimate. The Vietnam War was entirely illegitimate and could be argued to comprise a long-running war crime or a regimen of criminality against humanity. Reagan's inane four-day invasion of Grenada (ridiculously code-named Operation Urgent Fury) in 1983 was little more than a pathetic press-op to cover for cutting and running in Lebanon after the American embassy in Beirut was bombed a few months earlier. And the last two Gulf wars in the Middle East were simply errands for Big Oil (the second offering a nice a little side-dash for the massive naturally occurring lithium deposit in Afghanistan).

I try not to have a problem with folks saying "Thank you for your service" to veterans in person, on TV, radio, podcast, campaign trail, whatever, but the phrasing sometimes bothers me. Take this past Veterans Day, for example.

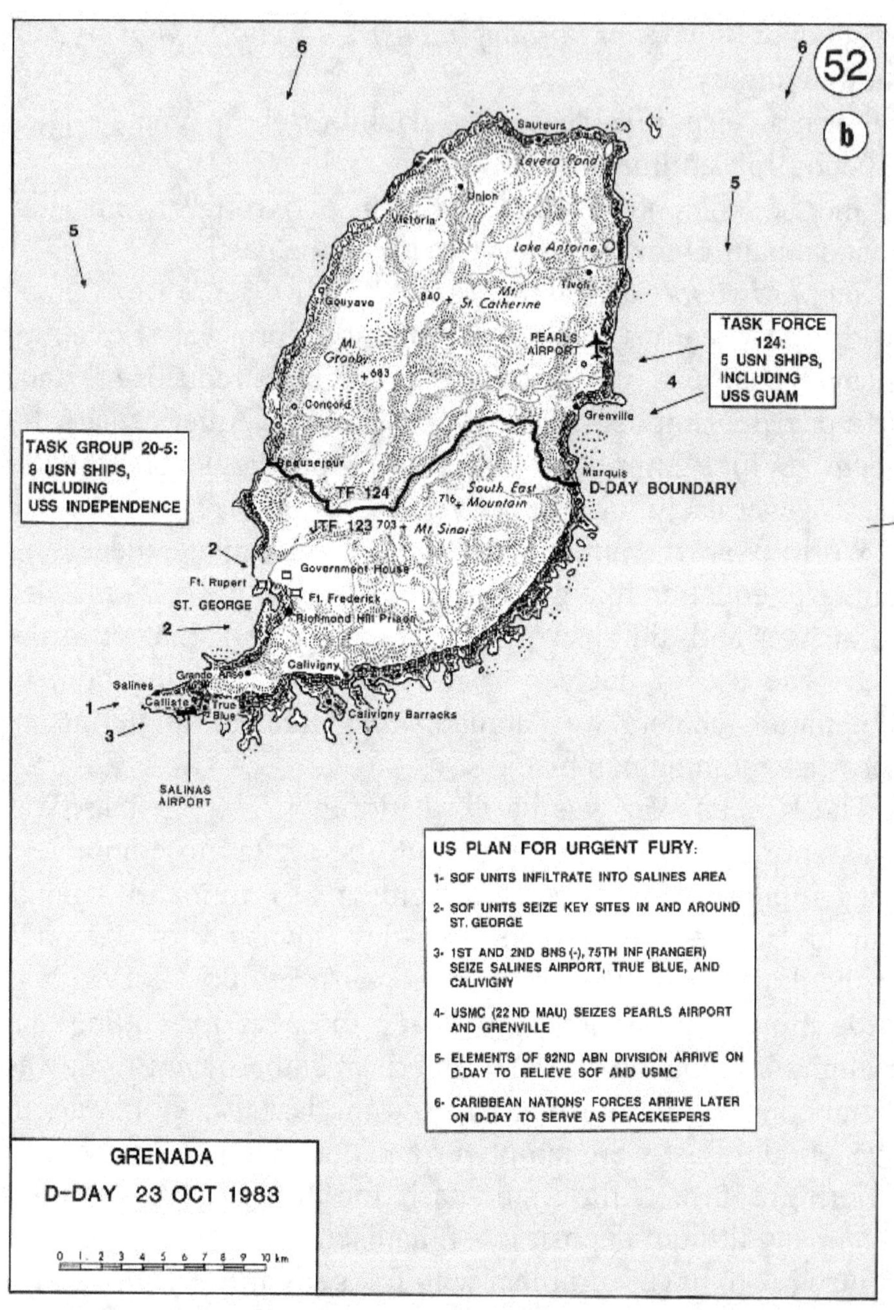

Operation Urgent Fury was little more than a "Mission-Accomplished" photo op for President Reagan, staged at the expense of a country the size of a small, midsize city in America. *Public Domain*

On one mildly interesting Texana page on a popular social platform, I encountered the image of a soldier with a caption featuring a proud proclamation: "Truly we stand on the shoulders of giants. My father in Vietnam, 1967."

This is where I get into trouble.

I appreciate the platform administrator's father's military service, but give me a break. If there were any giants in America's war against Vietnam, they were all Goliath. And Vietnam's David smote us in a poetic and Biblical sense.

In his farewell address sixty years ago, President Dwight D. Eisenhower warned against a new threat to American democracy: "In the councils of government, we must guard against the acquisition of unwarranted influence, whether sought or unsought, by the military-industrial complex. The potential for the disastrous rise of misplaced power exists and will persist."

We didn't heed Ike's warning, and, for the last three decades, warmongers have called the shots.

Ask JFK.

Ask MLK.

Hell, ask Barack Obama, the former *Droner-in-Chief.* Do you think he would have survived a stand against American Empire?

Lucky for the military-industrial complex, Americans have short memories and weren't real astute students of history to begin with—but our nation's belligerent foreign diplomacy makes us look like giant, ignorant, insufferable assholes who stood on the shoulders of more giant, ignorant, insufferable assholes.

Not heroes.

And this is where I get into more trouble.

With all due respect, most of the time when we thank our veterans for their "service," we're not really thanking them for their dedication, commitment, or sacrifice to worthy or even just causes. We're simply thanking them for putting their lives, limbs, and sanity on the line for our bullshit.

Shame on us.

Winning Isn't Anything If It's the Only Thing

February 2011 FLASHBACK

Winning isn't everything, it's the only thing.

In thousands of high school, college and pro locker rooms around the country, it is written. During hundreds of thousands of half-time speeches, motivational speaking seminars and out-of-town sales conventions, it is repeated. It defines American sports. It rationalizes American Capitalism. It's a dangerous lie perpetrated by the short-sighted.

I played high school and college sports. I understand that in a sweaty, brainwashed locker room, this quote makes a certain sense. But people take these mantras out into the world and live by them, and justify their unscrupulousness with them.

Winning is the only thing justifies gathering exceptional football players at well-to-do high schools by hook or crook. *Winning is the only thing* justifies future Super Bowl champions illegally filming opposing teams' defensive play-calling signals to ensure wins.

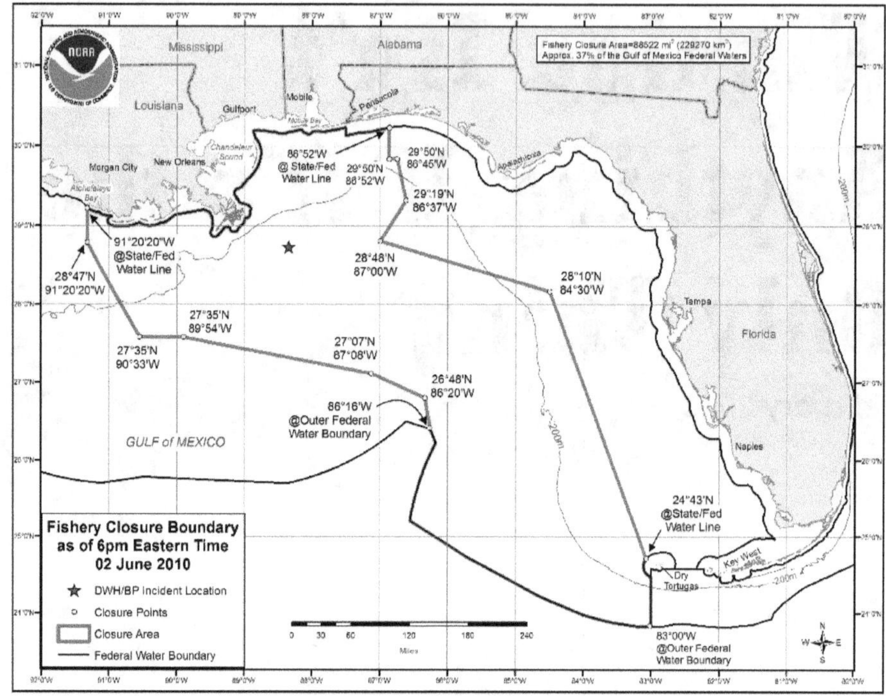

"Winning" often leads to inestimable casualties and immeasurable destructive effects. One example is the Deepwater Horizon oil spill. Above is the "Fishery Closure Boundary as of 6pm Eastern Time on June 2, 2010"[32] which encompassed 88,522 square miles. *Public domain.*

In the last several years we've seen sterling examples of all three. Sterling as in trophies. And the unscrupulous winning parties went largely unpunished, so the mantra was affirmed.

One of my uncles used to say that dollar signs were the only way to rack up points on the scoreboard of life, and I vehemently disagreed. But winning was the only thing for BP[33] on the Deepwater Horizon oil rig, and they were so anxious for another big win that they ignored failed pressure tests and skipped or skirted numerous safety precautions. Winning was also the only thing for big health insurance companies when they automatically challenged every medical

One of the signs carried at an Occupy protest in Washington, D.C. on November 19, 2011. *Wikipedia Commons.*[34]

claim they could to avoid losing revenue. And winning is the only thing that keeps natural gas magnates from coming clean about the current and long-term impacts of the "fracking" method of gas extraction, the induced seismicity it's led to, and the toxins it introduces into our water supplies.

Winning is the only thing is also what lead to the ludicrous legal rationale for "corporate" personhood. By winning the rights afforded under the law to natural persons for corporations, corporate entities established themselves as super players who—by the sheer fact of their numbers (human and monetary, but mostly monetary)—normal players or citizens couldn't compete with in the democratic process. And now the winning edge of corporate "persons" is felt in every election cycle when corporate donations determine our leadership and on a daily basis when corporate lobbyists—democratic representation on steroids—determine the "rules" or laws and/or "reffing" or governance.

So, let's set the record straight.

Winning isn't anything if it's the only thing.

If you and I aren't lining up on a level playing field, no one really wins. If the refs are in either of our pockets, the game isn't worth playing. And if one of us is juiced up on performance-enhancing drugs or profit-ensuring legalese, the scoreboard is a disgrace.

How long will we continue to embarrass ourselves? How long will conquests and wealth continue to justify cheating, inequality and kleptocracy?

How long will our hopes for the future continue to sit the bench while corporate lackeys, billionaire oligarchs and the dollar aristocracy make fortunes off our record-breaking losses?

Eat the Rich

November 1, 2023

On October 9, 2023, a complete human skeleton was found in the 12,000th block of Camp Bowie Blvd. West, near the western-most edge of Tarrant County. As the crow flies, about a mile from my home, just outside of Fort Worth, Texas.

Initially thought to be fake or maybe even a Halloween prank, the skeleton was confirmed to be of human origin, and the Sheriff's Department stated that the deceased's remains went unnoticed for so long because they lay in "an area not visible to business patrons or passing drivers."

Call me morbid, but I decided to find the site, because I was curious to see exactly where the skeleton had turned up. There was an old, abandoned Chevron gas station and convenience store in the vicinity, and the caretakers kept nailing up plywood over the store's broken windows to keep the homeless out. And, at some point—at least five years back—someone had spray-painted "EAT THE RICH" in two-foot-tall black letters on the plywood, and I wondered if that was where the body was found. It wasn't and I was relieved. The graffiti made me smile, and if that kind of graffiti makes you smile or gives you hope, you have to keep your head low.

But it was still heartening.

Image by author.

In 1875, barbed wire came to Texas. But back then, Texans were Texans—not ranch family bootlickers. So, as fast as the ranch families (whom many viewed as carpetbaggers) put the barbed wire up during the day, Texans snuck out and cut it down at night.

You see, real, authentic Texans considered the frontier to be communal property, especially since putting up fence-lines could be the difference between life and death. Barbed wire fencing denied public access and cut off crucial routes to critical water sources, for people and livestock. And water was more scarce then than it is now.

The battle against the partitioning off of the Texas frontier—which the good guys lost—became known as the Fence-Cutters War. A fascinating sequence of events in Texas history, it culminated in the ranchers poaching Texas Rangers to patrol their fence lines and, quite possibly, the development of the first IED. In 1888, a former Ranger rigged dynamite to blow up would-be fence-cutters. Heck, it was illegal to carry fence-cutters in your pocket in Austin until 1973.

But let's get back to the rich.

I don't know if many Texans knew who Jean Jacques Rousseau was in the late 1870s, but plenty were definitely of the same mind, even if Rousseau was a Genevan political philosopher who'd been dead for over a century. Rousseau's insights helped shape Age of Enlightenment in Europe, played a vital role in the French Revolution and largely contributed to the development of modern political, economic, and educational theory. Translated, of course, he once observed that "When the people have nothing more to eat, they will eat the rich."

In 1754, Rousseau wrote a treatise in response to a competition sponsored by the Academy of Dijon answering this prompt: "What is the origin of inequality among people, and is it authorized by natural law?" Rousseau's paper argued that private property is the source of inequality and it was later published as *Discourse on the Origin of Inequality.*

Portrait of Jean-Jacques Rousseau by Maurice Quentin de La Tour in 1753. *Public Domain*.[35]

He's perhaps better known as the author of *The Social Compact* (1762), but kudos to Rousseau on his first effort. No matter how much Social Darwinists argue that inequality is justified by natural law, it's a bald-faced, Capitalist lie (usually espoused or dimly groused about by balding, red-faced misers or aspiring misers). As American novelist and cultural critic Daniel Quinn cogently lays out in his *Ishmael* trilogy, this prevarication contributes to the destruction of the natural world. In *My Ishmael,* Quinn explains why, observing that the world is full of "Leavers" and "Takers". The primitive, tribal Leavers base their existence on sharing and sustainability; the Takers see themselves as rulers, consider the world their oyster, and insist the planet's resources are theirs for the taking (and hoarding).

The Texas fence-cutters were Leavers; the big ranchers were Takers—in fact, they often fenced in more than what was theirs. And as big as Texas is, it's simply a microcosm of the macrocosm. Billionaires and corporate conglomerates around the world are contemporary Takers.

This is why the nod to Rousseau at the boarded-up old Chevron station, now a derelict curiosity, made me smile. It meant that a few folks had paid attention in their history and social studies classes and probably remembered learning about the Sherman Antitrust Act and the Clayton Act, both of which were aimed at outlawing monopolies (*Howdy*, Amazon!) and preventing commercial entities from unfairly restraining or limiting competition (*Howdy*, Walmart!).

Most Republican and Democratic politicians seem to ignore these laws today. Which begs credulity, because the Sherman Act was signed fifteen years after barbed wire was introduced in Texas. And our political representatives are supposed to be in the business of looking after the American people—not the Trust Fund set.

All this to say, I sincerely doubt that the skeleton recently discovered at the 12,000th block of Camp Bowie West belonged to one of the Takers, the rich or one of Taylor Sheridan's put-upon, righteous *Yellowstone*s or King ranchers. I bet you dollars to donuts it was a lost Leaver.

They're much easier to prey upon and profit from preying upon.

And history will probably place that on our epitaph.

Mediocrity Burning

May 22, 2022

Two heavyweight Williams of Western lit walk into a bar.

The more prominent—William Shakespeare, still a household name centuries after his time—orders a mug of ale and quotes Antonio in *The Tempest*. "What's past is prologue," he says. The other William, his feet already propped up at a side table (their owner already sipping whisky), is William Faulkner, a Shakespeare of the American South but not a household name (except maybe in his home state of Mississippuh). He responds with a quote from *Requiem for a Nun*. "The past is never dead. It's not even past."

The bartender shrugs. "The more things change," he mumbles to himself, "the more they stay the same."

It's not really that funny, I know.

Especially in Texas.

But also across the country.

Things have indeed changed—but not for the *white* reasons.

Another weekend, another domestic white terrorist on the loose with an automatic weapon. Their motives blur together. Reverse discrimination, dwindling white population, the "Great Replacement" conspiracy, couldn't get a date, *blah, blah, blah*. Blathering examples of white mediocrity lashing

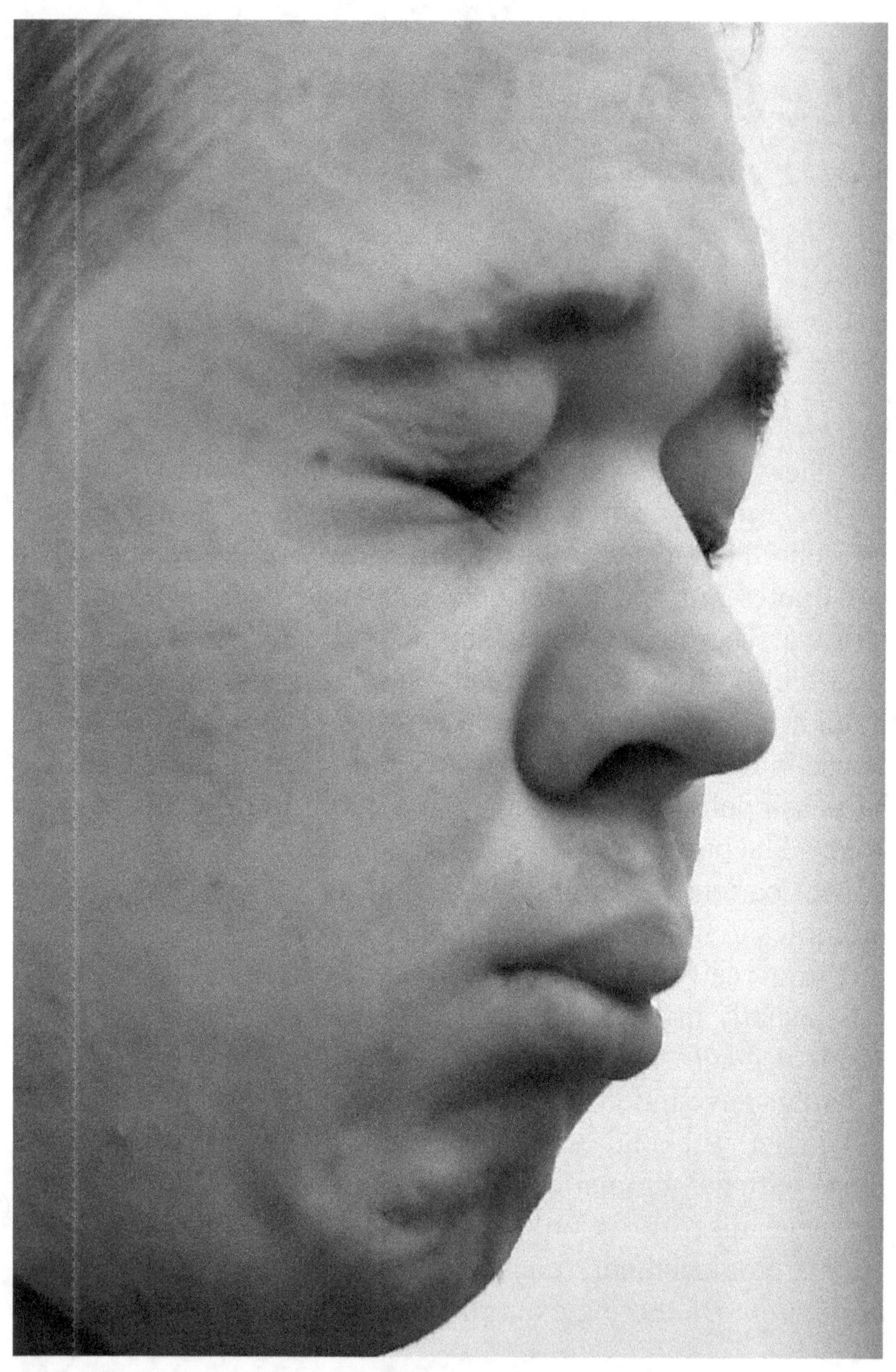

Mediocre white guy Kyle Rittenhouse "manning up" in court. *Public domain*.

out at a society that's trying to move past white male primacy and leaving vanilla lessers to feel, *well*, somehow less.

Their great-great-grandpappies never had to. It's the seminal line from the 1988 film *Mississippi Burning*. Gene Hackman's character tells a story about his father being embarrassed by the fact that a Black neighbor was able to afford a mule while his dad didn't have one. His dad's white neighbors ribbed him. The mule was poisoned and died and Hackman's character realizes his father had something to do with it. Hackman's character's dad's response sheds blinding white light on the shrewdest, most racially cataclysmic joke the Southern aristocracy played on average folks in the post-Civil War era: "If you're not any better than a nigger, son, who are you better than?"

Let's be honest.

Has anybody really taken a hard look at the white men and white teens who go on these shooting sprees? Sure, they obviously share beliefs and values (and grotesque thoughts and prayers) and, of course, Fox News worship. But have you really looked at them closely as individuals?

If you have (or do), a striking pattern begins to emerge.

The domestic white terrorists who commit these acts are an unremarkable parade of mediocrity, white guys who couldn't make the varsity football squad (or sat on the bench if they did), couldn't get dates (much less have or keep girlfriends), and are consigned to their high school yearbooks as dim or dumpy or goofy faces that no one would have remembered five years after graduation if not for their acts of racial hatred or domestic terror.

Twenty-one-year-old vanilla dud Dylann Roof killed nine African Americans at a Black Church in Charleston in 2015 and actually admitted to doing it because some girl he liked chose a Black kid over him. Twenty-one-year-old white dud

Patrick Crusius. *Art by author.*

Patrick Crusius drove more than eleven hours from Dallas to El Paso to kill twenty-three Hispanics (and wound twenty-three others) in 2019 (see *Appendix I* for his "manifesto"). Seventeen-year-old Anglo *dud* Kyle Rittenhouse crossed state lines and killed three Black Lives Matter protesters in 2020 to strike a blow for conservative white 'Murica, got away with it, and now wants move to Texas, where mediocre white "men" control most of the "Wango Tango".[36] And just last week a Conklin, New York, white dud named Payton Gendron drove 200 miles to kill eleven Black people in Buffalo, and, rumor has it, if he gets off, he'll also be coming to Texas, where, again, everyone knows how cowards eat the cabbage.

Back in their great- and great-great-grandpappies' days, you could kill men of color for even looking at white women. Or burn them at the stake for an insinuation or a whim—especially here in Texas. You could also rape their mothers, sisters, wives, and daughters without even having to stand trial. 'Murica was great for white male mediocrity in those days, and Dylann, Patrick, Kyle, and Payton would have fit right in.

Now, white male mediocrity can't even earn you a spot on the JV basketball bench, much less get you dates with cheerleaders. And legions of pathetic white men envision themselves put-upon Rosa Parkses because they can't get anybody to sit with them at the front of the bus. To make matters worse, the God of their old-time religion—who endowed them with the inalienable right to not only sit at the front of the bus but in the driver's seat of the latest BMW model—was never really even white. Their proverbial Word has been sullied, and their conjugal prospects are dwindling—that's what's ticking off mediocre white guys so much. They used to run things, and now they're just average, pale-skinned, irrelevant malcontents.

Their power is diminishing. The tick-tock, tick-tock of their time as unquestioned, uncontested white patriarchal superiors owning everything, controlling everything, and getting all the girls by privilege or primacy (voluntarily or by force) is running out, and they're being challenged to live up to America's progressive manifest destiny at a time when more and more of the available female population keeps swiping left on them.

It's a Shakespearian tragedy. They're Faulknerian footnotes.

*Cue the mediocre white boys nodding along with Tucker Carlson while they peruse gun catalogs.

Texit Would Be a Wreck

June 29, 2022

I recently had a fender-bender smack-dab in the middle of Camp Bowie Boulevard, a minor collision that left the tail ends of both vehicles hanging out into the left lanes of the east- and westbound traffic.

No one slowed down, so I got out of my truck to wave off the traffic on the other vehicle's side, and the other driver, a Latina, pulled onto the road I'd come from. I returned to my truck and parked behind her.

Unbeknownst to me, a Fort Worth police patrol car had arrived at the Sonic on that side road. The officer was responding to a call there, but he didn't see our collision. He simply came over to make sure we were OK. The Latina and I were both fine, and so was her toddler, who had been properly strapped into a car-seat in her back seat. The officer had to finish addressing the incident at Sonic, but he took our license and insurance info.

The Latina and the child got back into her car, and she made a phone call. When the conversation ended, I walked up to her window. We exchanged phone numbers, and she seemed anxious. The car and the insurance were in her father's name. I asked her if everything was OK. She smiled and nodded, but I could tell she was concerned.

At that point, I became anxious. What if she had a warrant? What if she was an immigrant and didn't have her papers?

The officer hadn't seen the collision and couldn't assess blame. The insurance companies would battle it out. If the officer hadn't been responding to another call, he wouldn't have engaged us or asked for our licenses or insurance at all. I was suddenly concerned.

I walked over to the Sonic and asked the officer if he had a prybar I could use to try to bend my fender back out. He didn't, but he said he'd be with us in a minute. As I walked back to our parked vehicles, I realized why I was concerned. The last thing I wanted to see was a young woman separated from her child for a fender-bender. If the officer returned and the Latina had a warrant or an expired green card, our mishap might result in her arrest. I didn't exactly have flashbacks of brown children locked in cages at the Texas/Mexico border, but I knew with absolute certainty I couldn't trust the laws of my state or my fellow Texans' attitudes toward immigrants. And I knew I'd rather err on the side of human decency than Texas injustice.

I asked the Latina if she cared whether or not we included the officer in any kind of report. She said she'd rather not, unsuccessfully attempting to conceal her anxiety. I revisited the officer at the Sonic and told him that the Latina and I had exchanged info and that we didn't require his assistance. He said her driver's license was expired.

"You look like you got your hands full here," I said, nodding at the Sonic. "We're OK."

"You sure?" he asked.

COME AND TEXIT

Art by author.

"Positive," I replied, and he returned my license and walked over and spoke with the Latina briefly.

After the police officer departed, the Latina texted me to make sure I was OK. I assured her I was.

I reported the accident, and my insurance company told me to take my truck to a collision repair center actually owned by a sitting Republican U.S. Congressman. Sheesh, I thought, a politician who profited politically off brown children being locked up in cages would now profit from my accident. It didn't thrill me, but I needed my truck repaired.

A week after I dropped it off, I received a call from one of the collision center's supervisors telling me that the truck was torn down but the replacement parts were another three weeks out.

"Ever since Biden got elected," he said, "we're having all kinds of problems."

At that point, I'd had enough. "If you think the election of President Biden is what's causing supply shortages, then you haven't got two brain cells left to rub together. The supply issues started during COVID conditions under the previous administration."

Silence.

I knew he'd misread my unmistakable Southern drawl and presumed too much. And I realized I'd just irresponsibly mouthed off to the guy in charge of fixing my truck.

"But this isn't about politics," I told him. "I understand."

We finished the conversation cordially, but I was frustrated.

What happened to Texas, and what's wrong with Texans? Is there any escape from conservative small-mindedness now? *Doesn't it permeate every aspect of our culture and manifest itself as bigotry, chauvinism, greed, and ignorance at every turn?*

I suddenly recalled President George W. Bush's remarks a couple of weeks after the Twin Towers fell in New York City in 2001. "They hate us for our freedoms," he said.

It was laughable then, of course. They "hated" us because we routinely and covertly undermine their governments and overtly try to bomb them back to the Middle Ages for Big Oil. Bush's comment was ludicrous then, but it's spot on now—about us.

We really do seem to "hate us for our freedoms." We hate fair elections, voting rights, health care, freedom of religion, freedom of speech, and education in general. We hate Muslims, LGBTQ+, Mexicans, Mexican Americans, Asians, immigrants, librarians, and Black people—unless they play football, basketball, or run track (and only then if they don't kneel during the national anthem for a nation we hardly consider ourselves a part of). We care more about fossil fuels than fresh water, and we fight more for the rights of disturbed white males who envision themselves as the Punisher than any innocent Texas girl's sovereignty over her own body.

Everything's not bigger in Texas.

We're a small-minded state full of small-minded, ignorant people. We despise American freedoms and ideals so much that we're hardly even worthy of them anymore. And the new *Redophile* political platform in Texas capitalizes on this perversity, delegitimizing the results of the 2020 presidential election and reiterating the Lone Star state's right to secede from the United States.

Which sounds great if we're aspiring to a Lone Star civil war or an imbecilic lapse into a bloviating banana republic (with an emphasis on already having gone fricking bananas!).

But Texit wouldn't be a secession. It would be a *cessation* of human rights and human dignity for a large part of the population.

Home on the (Gun) Range

August 3, 2022

In an era when the lines seem starker between black and white, good and bad, right and wrong, and even strong and weak, I have a guilty pleasure. I have a reliable go-to that seems especially fitting, specifically in regards to where we stand today in Texas. Our home on the range is now a gun range.

Sure, we watch coverage of or read the stories about road rage and code rage and lament lapses of goaded rage, and we complain about the innocent men, women, and children dying in schools, grocery stores, churches, and other public spaces, and our political representatives carefully monitor our collective pulse on the issue and appear to dabble in gun control legislation. There's no denying that. But are firearms the real problem?

Are my liberal friends listening (and ready to pounce)?

I'll say it again. *Are firearms the real problem?*

Or are they just a deadly symptom?

Are we not a culture obsessed with criminality and murder sprees? Netflix, Amazon, HBO, Vudu, Hulu — check out their most popular programming, especially for men and young men. *Are we not entertained?*

Vengeance sells. Righteous and even pseudo-righteous indignation lines the pockets of conservative and liberal progenitors of gratuitous violence alike. And the majority of us buy guns with nobody in particular to fire at. We're simply compelled by streaming services and infotainment to be prepared.

We have to be ready to protect our land or our family or our way of life. Most of us don't have much of a life, and very few of us have lives that someone else would want to take or even take on. But we are obsessed with vigilance.

Can't get a date, can't get laid, or compete with persons of color? Can't hold our sexist, chauvinist, racist, or pseudo-righteous heads up with pride? Is someone disrespecting us or challenging our scam or our hustle or our familial excess or our personal indulgences? Or threatening the deviants in our family?

(And this for my objecting liberal friends.) What would James Gandolfini's character in *The Sopranos* do? What would Bryan Cranston's character in *Breaking Bad* do? What would Jason Bateman's character in *Ozark* do? What about Kevin Costner's character in *Yellowstone*?

Do I even have to ask?

In America, the good, the semi-good, and even the serially sometimes good solve their problems with guns—*and we all like to watch.* And we prefer the bad guys (or the others we perceive as bad or a threat to our badness) dead. It's box office gold. It's a tickertape, tuxedo honor at the Oscars and parade-worthy, name-a-traffic-thoroughfare-after, key-to-the-city courage practically everywhere else. It's the American way, especially of late.

Gregory Peck as "Atticus Finch" in *To Kill A Mockingbird* (1962). *Public domain.*

But I look around, and I can't help but think of my go-to. It's also black and white. It's the 1962 film version of *To Kill a Mockingbird*.

Don't get me wrong. I love Harper Lee's book. I've read it four or five times at least. But for me, the face of Atticus Finch is always Gregory Peck. A white, male protagonist trying to do what's right. A white lawyer seeking justice, regardless of the time period or the all-white male jury. A white man challenging an oppressive Jim Crow atmosphere that pervades every aspect of his community in a 1962 film—*isn't it amazing how far we haven't come?*

I don't think many Americans remember the film, but perhaps they deserve some slack. It came out 60 years ago. And *To Kill a Mockingbird* was a little choo-choo train that thought it could. And it did, at least for a while.

Do any of y'all remember Peck as Atticus Finch? Did you know he won the Academy Award for best actor for that role?

Did you know, in fact, that—according to the American Film Institute's first 100 years of film list of the greatest motion picture heroes of all time—Gregory Peck's Finch is ranked No. 1? That's No. 1, ahead of Harrison Ford's Indiana Jones, Sean Connery's James Bond (Dr. No), Humphrey Bogart's Rick Blaine (*Casablanca*), and Gary Cooper's Marshall Kane (*High Noon*). And obviously Bruce Willis' John McLane in *Die Hard*, Sylvester Stallone in *Rambo, Die Hard 5* (*A Good Day to Die Hard*), *Rambo 5* (*Rambo: Last Blood*), and the upcoming buddy spinoff, *Die Hambo: Let's Make a Billion Dollars* (fleecing bloodbath-addicted halfwits).

Atticus Finch's kids were threatened. Another white man even spat in his face. Dirty Harry wouldn't have stood for that. The Duke wouldn't have taken that lying down, and neither would have Clint Eastwood, Liam Neeson, Tom Cruise, Arnold Schwarzenegger, or Matt Damon—they would have popped a cap in someone's ass or aired out somebody's skull. We're Americans, *dammit!*

Atticus Finch's courage was quiet and dignified. Atticus Finch's courage was plain and softspoken.

Atticus Finch didn't have a pistol, and he used his shotgun only to kill a rabid dog—and the canine's rabies was symbolic of ignorance and ignorant rabidity in general.

It seems bizarre now, right?

These days, our most rabidly ignorant friends and neighbors are stockpiling guns and strapping up to go to Dairy Queen. *What happened to us?*

We have chances to be Atticus Finches all the time, but we choose "God and Guns" over real guts and prospective death-dealing over empathy and human decency.

Do we have any real courage or dignity left?

The recent profligacy of gun ranges is not reassuring.

Jiminy Hegemony

January 13, 2022

As a native Texan, I used to be fairly oblivious to outside perceptions of my home state. I never watched a single episode of *Dallas*, for example, but when I visited Western Europe in the summer of 1984, I was surprised that practically everyone I met assumed I owned horses and oil wells. Then, the following summer, when some New York City girls saw me surfing in Hawaii, they were surprised to learn I hailed from the Lone Star State. They condescendingly remarked that they thought all Texans were farmers. Later, in college, one of my favorite professors (from the upper Midwest) found my Texas drawl so off-putting that I was mildly scolded. "You're going to be famous someday," the professor said. "You need to learn how to speak English."

When I backpacked through Europe in 1994 with shoulder-length dreadlocks and my Texas drawl still intact (if not even more pronounced), many Europeans thought my accent was Australian and assumed I was an Aussie. And every Aussie I met—themselves hailing from a "renegade" state—quickly recognized in me a kindred spirit.

The years passed, and I still remained relatively oblivious to outsider speculation. We'd had Ann Richards as governor and still had Molly Ivins. George W. Bush was a horrendous jagaloon, but voices with Molly's mettle laid him bare for all to see. Sheesh, Texas had even been home to American Atheist Madalyn Murray O'Hair, and when I was young, Cowtown was a mecca for famous gay folks, including transplanted tennis legend Martina Navratilova, world-renowned pianist Van Cliburn, and heirless business magnate Sid Richardson (the latter two deceased), some of whose vast wealth fell to contemporary business legends, the Bass brothers. These three wildly visible LGBTQ-before-LGBTQ-was-cool figures never came out, but plenty of people knew. It just wasn't a big deal.

Further back, native Texan and 34th U.S. President Dwight D. Eisenhower had helped lead us to victory in WWII but quite pointedly called out the American military-industrial complex in his farewell address. Native Texan and Thirty-sixth U.S. President Lyndon Baines Johnson—the war in Vietnam notwithstanding—was the most progressive president in American history, responsible for an unprecedented amount of legislation designed to protect our air, water, and wilderness, expand quality-of-life initiatives, improve education, create Headstart, fight poverty, establish racial equality and improve workplace safety.

Unbelievable now, right? But it's true.

In 1963, LBJ signed the Clean Air Act, the Higher Education Facilities Act, and the Vocational Education Act. In 1964, LBJ signed the Civil Rights Act, the Urban Mass Transportation Act, the Wilderness Act, the Nurse Training Act, the Food Stamp Act, the Economic Opportunity Act, and the Housing Act. In 1965, LBJ signed the Higher Education Act, the Older Americans Act (the first federal initiative created to provide comprehensive services for older adults), the Social Security Act of 1965 (which established Medicare), the Voting Rights Act, and the Immigration and Nationality Services Act. In

People forget that Texan Lyndon Baines Johnson, 36th President of the United States, was the most progressive president in American history. This picture was taken in 1972, the year before his death. *Public domain.*

1966, LBJ signed the Animal Welfare Act and the Freedom of Information Act (FOIA). In 1967, LBJ signed the Age Discrimination in Employment Act and the Public Broadcasting Act (creating NPR). In 1968, LBJ signed the Bilingual Education Act (the first U.S. federal legislation addressing the needs of limited English-speaking ability students), a second Civil Rights Act, and the Gun Control Act (banning mail-order sales of rifles and shotguns and prohibiting most felons, drug users, and people found mentally incompetent from buying guns).

Let me restate: *The most powerful, effective progressive in American history was a Texan.*

And now his home state is one of the most backwards places on the planet.

It's depressing.

Ann and Molly are gone, and many of our neighbors mumble "abomination" under their breaths when they see homosexuals. Texas has as many God-botherers as anywhere else in the country, and the Lone Star State attracts military-industrial profiteers like bees to honey. And my old Aussie mates live in a country where gun laws have evolved, not devolved.

For my part—like most Texans—I still don't have any horses or oil wells or do much farming. I still, however, talk like a Texan and probably exhibit at least the half-swagger of someone oafishly belligerent—like many of my fellow Texans. I came closer to being infamous than famous and, now aged, more resemble a character on Duck Dynasty than a surfer or a world traveler. I still live in Texas, but I hardly recognize my state. I still consider myself a Texan, but I am appalled by so many Texans who don't know or simply ignore their own history.

In Lone Star vernacular, the parlor lights are on, but no one's home. And half the folks I meet are several bricks shy of a load.

Lately, we look like superficial, xenophobic morons who never produced an LBJ or Eisenhower, much less an Ann or Molly. Nobody with any real standards wants us in their bedrooms, bathrooms, or classrooms. Our men are all hat, and we treat our women like chattel. We're a pathetic caricature of independence and bravery and all the lies the Alamo was always based on. And we're like an uber-obtuse exercise in word association.

If someone says "good," we say "bad." If someone says "scientist," we say "liar." If someone says "evil," we say "necessary." If someone says "black," we say "blue." If someone says "white," we say "right." If someone says "oil," we shout "Hallelujah, pass the global warming!" And if someone says "woman" (or, heaven forbid, "a woman's sovereignty of her own body"), we respond with a sneering, faux-righteous "not on my watch."

Beloved Lone Star hero Willie Nelson used to say, "I'm from Texas, and one of the reasons I like Texas is because there's no one in control." But now Willie's simply mistaken.

Red-state, white, male hegemony is where we're at—and we seem to like it that way.

Today we ban honest books and refuse to punish (much less censure) dishonest, corrupt politicians. Today, Texans no longer lead—Texas is a breeding ground for fear and ignorance and moral cowards. And today, though we didn't succeed at all as our own country or separate republic, we ludicrously threaten to secede more than we say the "Pledge of Allegiance."

Hell, this past year Texas conservatives did their batshit-crazy best to gerrymander the state back to the middle-19th century, hoping to make us look like the Great White Hope for America in the 21st century, but to the rest of the world—and anyone paying attention in this country—we look more like a stunted confederacy of vaccs hoaxers, Roe-revokers, defiant Jim Crow stokers, and reinstate-Scopes-Monkey-decision coaxers. We're not a Great White Hope.

We're a dull, ignorant gaggle of grating, white-supremacist, misogynist dolts.

Clarity Lacking in Modern Society

Clarity is a primitive, creeping thing. It slithers beneath our ignorance. It slinks behind out lust. It crouches around the corners we cut. It bleeds in the eyes of those we betray. Only in the forgotten, yellowing pages of our best literature does it stand apparent, aggressive and demanding acknowledgement.

In our society, clarity is a dangerous fugitive, but we never hunt it down or indict it. We know that such proceedings would be unprofitable—that the only acceptable verdict would be criminal—so we grant it perpetual amnesty on the presumption of banishment.

Our government goes to especially great lengths to avoid it (as its testimony would expose the gangrenous decay that's infected the profuse underside of America's bureaucratic paunch). If elusion is impossible, politicians try to cover it up; if a cover-up is impossible, special operatives pacify it.

Organized religions lack government's tact. In many cases, before they even hear or see it, they condemn or ban it. And if they can corner it and get their hands on it, they either strap it to a stake, perform a scurrilous inquisition and burn it; or they

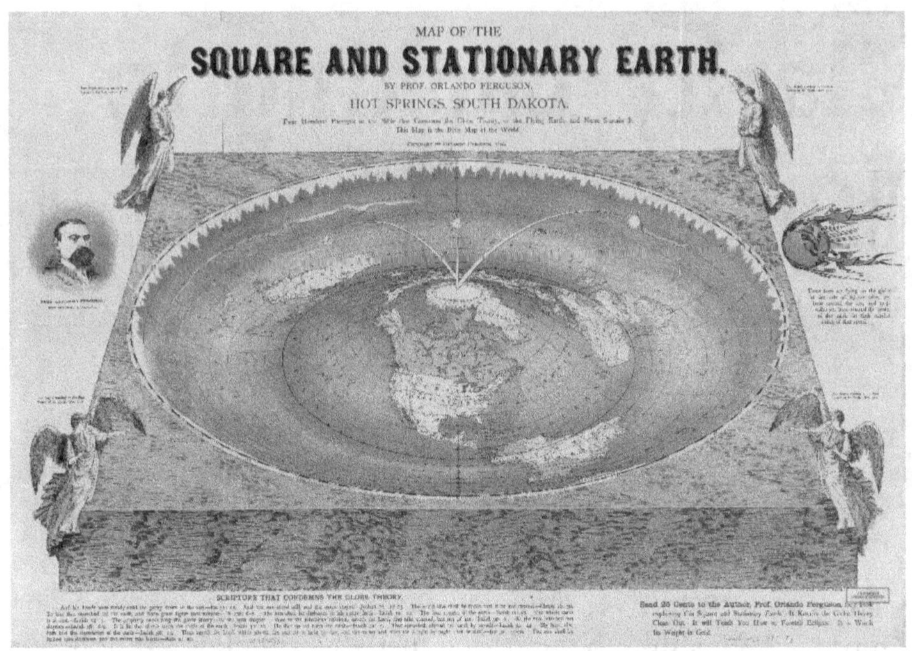

Hardly anything in American society fosters or encourages clarity, and it's been that way for a long time. "Map of the square and stationary Earth" (1893), *Library of Congress*.

shackle it to a rack and demand that it renounces itself. If it refuses to repent, they stretch it or twist it until it's vague enough to incorporate in their doctrines.

Big business also disfigures it, but more with embroidery and embellishment. Industrialists staple a smile on its face and dab a sparkle in its eye, and then Xerox it—its happy likeness is placed strategically throughout markets to convince you you're someone you're not and make you buy things you don't need.

The general population hides from it, burrowing silently into rabbit holes of desire and decadence at even the hint of its approach. We use alcohol and drugs to drown it. We use television and music to distract ourselves from it. We use love and hate to disavow it.

Who can blame us?

Clarity obstructs political injustice and quits governmental waste; clarity scoffs at corporate data and threatens Capitalist unscrupulousness. Clarity challenges our *holey* Scriptures and endangers the church's glorious sinecure. Clarity disembowels our sunny myths and spotlights our glaring half-measures. Clarity spits on our "freedom and justice for all" platitudes and regurgitates our baseball, hot dogs and apple pie.

Clarity is a primitive, creeping thing that exacts redemption, atonement. It haunts our conscience. It terrifies us. Those who possess it are either investigated as threats or persecuted as aberrations. Those who brandish it are exorcised, crucified or assassinated.

So, it is a good thing we avoid it, ignore it and flee from it madly. Clarity is clearness, distinctness—purity—its very acquaintance would undermine the justifications for most of our very ways of life.

Surely life is more important than wrong or right.

Sometimes I wonder what would happen if tomorrow clarity descended upon us relentlessly, unforgivably; but deep inside I'm afraid I already have the answer. Somewhere in the back of my brain, beneath the clean, grey clouds, lie angry black and white extremes and an altruistic, indignant voice that screams for reform and reckoning.

When I listen too closely, it tells me we are lost. It says we're so far off that, if tomorrow, all the questions were answered and the facts were known—about our glories and glamours and goods and gods, and the incredible, astounding pile of sanctimonious, superficial, superfluous gout we call the system—mankind would collapse in and on itself. It says we're so far gone that facing the truth would create a vacuum, and the dark, motionless void that is humankind's soul would suck itself into an indefatigable black hole.

Thank God for TV, drugs and sex!?

Gen X-ed

October 20, 2021

Big hair, turned-up collars, Members Only jackets, Swatches, New Kids on the Block. There were gobs of ridiculousness in the 1980s. Too much to list really.

It wasn't all "totally awesome." In fact, in many ways it was unequivocally absurd.

Over the last century, seven decades were defined by war. Another two were given meaning by Prohibition or a great depression. The 1980s were the only decade in the last ten that wasn't defined by any of the three—unless you count the War on Drugs, which was initiated by Richard Nixon in 1971 but more infamously waged by Nancy Reagan's "Just Say No" campaign. But no one took that seriously (especially the CIA). The most traumatic thing that happened in the '80s was probably New Coke. The rising generations of the other nine decades had the crux of their angst defined for them. We were left to our own devices.

Our elders called us Generation X or Gen X, and there was something to this. In algebraic terms, we were an unknown quantity. We seemed directionless, ambitionless. Without a war or cataclysmic social or economic fiasco to suffer through or rail against, we had the luxury of looking around and taking note of things. Usually superficially, but still. There was no

A doofus for all seasons, Ronald Reagan was one of the biggest phonies of the Eighties. *Public domain.*

movement or spirit-crushing calamity to sway us from what was right in front of us. It was a blessing and a curse.

For those of us who were paying attention, there was this incredible sense that everything was wrong or going wrong. Not one thing or one issue. But everything.

Capitalism, corporatism, Reagan, famine, AIDS, ozone depletion—Holden Caufield was only a third right. The world of adults wasn't just phony. It was irresponsible and dangerous. The world faced a thousand reckonings, none of which were our doing, and we deeply resented the inherited, irretrievable missteps, the resultant, impending disasters, and the day the bill for the causative idiocy and irresponsibility would come due. It seemed a long way off, but it wasn't. And the extraordinary, horrifying question that occurred to us even then was what we would do when we were adults.

In *The Breakfast Club* (1985), the most popular cinematic examination of Gen X during this period, every high school participant's stint in detention was due to some form of parental obliviousness, neglect, or specific parentally encouraged oafishness. And after each kid shares their reason for being there, Emilio Estevez's character honestly and poignantly says, "My god, are we gonna be like our parents?"

Now, for the adults and grownups of the period who observed our generation from without, pay special attention. No matter how knuckleheaded or pea-brained any of us may have seemed at the time, all of our ears perked up at the Emilio character's interrogative. And what followed.

Molly Ringwald's character says, "Not me. Ever."

Not me. Ever.

Then Ally Sheedy's character breaks the spell with a statement most of us resented (in every cell of our being):

"It's unavoidable. It just happens. When you grow up, your heart dies."

This is how the real world appeared to us. And our parents' recipe for success and personal fulfillment was following in their heartless footsteps.

We were the first generation raised with video games and arguably the first generation of kids relentlessly subjected to corporate marketing strategies designed to make us complacent little materialists. To those of us who withstood these campaigns with some semblance of sentience intact, the "real" world (as our elders put it) was a sad compromise, a big sellout. Adulthood was a minefield. And the rat race was[37] a shameless, voluntary evil.

No one stated our distaste for Capitalism more succinctly or

Molly Ringwold and Judd Nelson in Gen X classic, *The Breakfast Club*. Courtesy of *Corpus Christi Caller-Times*, February 27, 1985.

humorously than "Lloyd Dobler", John Cusack's character in another '80s classic, *Say Anything* (1989). When asked by his romantic interest's father what he planned to do after high school, he speculates candidly, "I don't want to sell anything, buy anything, or process anything as a career. I don't want to sell anything bought or processed or buy anything sold or processed or process anything sold, bought, or processed or repair anything sold, bought, or processed."

Amen, Dobler. *Amen.*[38]

Or at least that's what our sentiment was then.

Somewhere along the way, however, we forgot. Or, as our well-meaning parents put it, we "grew up."

It was a lie then, and it's a lie now.

Actor John Cusack. *Courtesy of WKT Public Relations.*

Decent, reasonable adults don't disenfranchise their neighbors for political gain. Fair-minded folks don't sell out fellow citizens for higher profit margins or inflated stock options. Practical-minded grownups don't sacrifice their children's future well-being for shallow, short-term gratifications. And responsible, rational human beings don't base their economy on gambled derivatives, resource speculation, or opportunistic wars to keep Big Oil—and the biggest consumer of oil and gas on the planet, the U.S. military-industrial complex—chugging forward and belching death.

Americans haven't been adults about anything for years, but perhaps the closest we came to it was in the '80s when Gen Xers looked around and said, "Wow. This is fucked up."

The revelation was drilled out of us in short order.

Love him or hate him, Barack Obama was the first Gen-X president, and he brought a mild version of this sensibility to the job. He moved the dial a little, but he was followed by a rabidly backward Baby Boomer and then his own former vice president, a tepid, middle-of-the-road Boomer dealing with a stupefyingly divisive pandemic.

Now, of course, we're the "grownups."

And we have become our parents. We're buying and selling and processing lies, staunching our idealism, dooming our children's future, and defiling the fierce, innocent soul of our generation. If our hearts aren't dead, they're dying. We willfully embrace falsehoods and invest in them. So much so that we can longer make sense of our lives outside the careful confines of ignorance and wishful prevarication.

As teenagers, we weren't impressed. As adults we're not impressive.

It's too bad.

We had such promise.

Fox Muzak

Sometimes you find hope where there is none.

It rarely comes from the truth or even people you admire, respect, or love. The truth these days is unpleasant. And our circle of intimates and quasi-intimates is constantly impressed upon by advertising, psychologists, and self-help gurus to make us or keep us happy.

I wasn't looking for truth last Saturday. It was just a tune, a song, and not even a protest song. It was more like a giant, brave "Fuck you" to me, my generation, and generations of the recent past. *Rolling Stone* describes the Yeah Yeah Yeahs' "Spitting Off the Edge of the World" as "a smoldering cut" that "builds to a massive peak filled with crashing drums and keening guitar riffs," but it's more than that. And it addresses us—me and you—in the first line: "Cowards, here's the sun / So bow your heads."

And it doesn't let up:

> *In the absence of bombs*
> *Draw your breath*
> *Dark, dark places shall be none*
> *She's melting houses of gold*
> *And the kids cry out*
> *We're spitting off the edge of the world*

Ouch!

We may not be paying attention, but someone is. And though all the blame or fault for the current state of things may not be ours to shoulder alone, I understand why so many of us remain oblivious to what's happening. It has an interesting history.

Elevator music, more commonly referred to as Muzak, became in vogue a century ago this year. The original purpose of Muzak was to calm passengers who were fearful of riding in elevators. The mechanical lurch of the strange, artificial ascent. The startling, obverse sensation of falling or rising in slow motion. It was all new at the time.

The increasing use of elevator Muzak is a near-perfect metaphor to explain what just happened in the recent Lone Star election cycle. And the last several, in fact.

A couple of weeks ago, I was passing through East Texas doing research. It was late, and I stopped at the first Tex-Mex place I saw in Lufkin. It was a great little spot with four TV screens. Two were tuned to the Astros (*yay!*). Two were set on Fox News. The baseball game was silent, and the Fox News broadcast was a low drone.

I was suddenly certain that Republicans would remain in power in Texas come November 8, because I had the sinking suspicion that the scene in this Tex-Mex eatery was being ceaselessly replicated in small-town restaurants across the state leading up to Election Day. Conservatives have been busy and meticulous. Many of these areas often don't have easy access to NPR, much less MSNBC, but they've always got Fox News. It's a staple of their existence.

That's the genius of it. Though inane and existentially perverse, Fox News is Muzak for the apocalypse. And the idea for it originated a half-century ago.

By the early 1970s, our war in Vietnam was wildly unpopular. The nationwide protests of the late 1960s and early '70s had been incredibly successful, and the public's opinion of President Richard Nixon and the conflict had begun to fluctuate in ways that made the administration uncomfortable. Simply put, the problem was that Nixon wasn't doing what he promised (i.e., getting the United States out of Vietnam), and his charade was complicated by the Kent State shootings and other harrowing, ugly optics. But a new media advisor helped Nixon weather the storm and win reelection in 1972.

His name was Roger Ailes.

For the former Fox News founder and the Nixon administration, the problem was never what Nixon was doing wrong or the promises he refused to deliver on. It was how what he was doing was being reported by the American media. And during the course of the summer of 1970, a memo titled "A Plan for Putting the GOP on the News" was circulated. The memo was discovered by John Cook at *Gawker* in 2011. Here is a telling excerpt from this 50-year-old Republican manifesto:

Today, television news is watched more often than people read newspapers, than people listen to the radio, than people read or gather from any other form of communication. The reason: People are lazy. With television you just sit—watch—listen. The thinking is done for you.

Ailes' handwritten notes are all over the memo, and it outlines a plan hatched between the Nixon White House and Ailes to coordinate the dissemination of pro-Republican "news" to television networks around the country.

President Nixon and Roger Ailes during the 1968 Nixon presidential campaign. *Public domain.*

Long before Ailes became the nefarious progenitor of Fox News and Fox Television Stations, his acknowledged difficulty with the American media was not that it was too liberal or couldn't be trusted or was even "lamestream." It was simply that journalists were doing their job and the coverage of the Nixon Administration's general failings and contemptible strategies was unfavorable, particularly where the unpopular war was concerned. White House staffers like Ailes (and Dick Cheney and Donald Rumsfeld) considered Nixon's unscrupulous tactics irrelevant. They were simply concerned with the American public's perception of them.

The Vietnam War was considered the first "TV war," and LBJ and Nixon both claimed that TV coverage hurt the American military effort. The images of the dead and wounded soldiers and body bags during the LBJ and Nixon administrations were disturbing and demoralizing. And the footage of the antiwar protests and the assault and murder of antiwar protesters during the Nixon administration were unequivocally damning, in the same way the images of the beating of Civil Rights protesters had been in years previous.

Ailes essentially proposed a "GOP TV" strategy, and though it took twentysomething years and the repeal of the Fairness Doctrine to accomplish, once Ailes and Rupert Murdoch pulled it off, America changed.

If broad swathes of the provincial U.S. citizenry didn't like what responsible journalists were reporting, they had a friend they could turn to, a "news" source that would filter out unwanted criticism, promote conventional perspectives, manufacture tacit consent (and conformity), and limit and censor authentic reporting that challenged complacency and established mores. Witch hunts could be perpetrated and never seriously condemned. Military conflicts predicated on outright prevarications could be waged. Journalism hazardous to staid principles and prescribed dogma could be mitigated. TV that portrayed war efforts in unflattering lights could be mitigated. And a viewership that knew why or knew better could also be mitigated. And Ailes' successful incarnation of GOP TV changed everything, even eventually wooing many aging '60s antiwar protesters—who had previously despised almost everything about Nixon's machinations—into the fold.

The undeniable genius of Roger Ailes was that he knew then what we're finding out now: If Fox News had been around in the early 1970s, the war in Vietnam would not have ended. It might have gone on and on like the war in Afghanistan. The Nixon presidency would not have been mortally wounded by Watergate, and Nixon himself wouldn't have been forced to resign in disgrace.

Roger Ailes in 2013. *Public Domain.*

Locally, Fox News would help vapid goober gubernatorial candidate George W. Bush and his hatchet man Karl Rove underhandedly torpedo wildly popular incumbent Texas Governor Ann Richards, and the leadership of the Lone Star

State since then has been little more than the oafish natterings of an arrogant Republican sausage factory, mostly benefiting all things straight, white, and male and obligatorily prostrate to lick the boots of petroleum profiteers and shameless right-wing billionaires.

The once mythic, legendary Texas free for all—independent, mysterious, unpredictable, and high-flying—is now a sad monument to cowardly conservative obviousness, sinking instead of rising and certainly more diminutive in spirit and stature than it was in the late 20th century. Texas is a national and international embarrassment. We offer wonderful institutes of higher education that most of us—including college graduates—manage to emerge from without being educated and flatly ignore except on gameday. We have a wealth of cultural diversity, but this diversity is ignored by our leadership and perpetually undermined by unconstitutional gerrymandering regimes, voter suppression and intimidation, false accusations of voter fraud, and good, old-fashioned economic exclusivity.

It's a sorry, pathetic state of affairs, but that's the way the seeming majority of our voting populous prefers it, so the only things really bigger in Texas these days are ignorance, xenophobia, historical amnesia, and white fragility. And they're seemingly unassailable totems of a toxic social hellscape.

So . . . *why do we stand for it?*

That's easy.

Fox News Muzak.

Texans are suffering. Texans are being murdered en masse by Fox News devotees. And Fox News viewers from other states—some who have gotten away with murdering American protesters—are moving to Texas to feel more at home. Texans also made up a large part of the contingent that stormed the U.S. Capitol on January 6, 2021.

But you get only superficial treatment of these stories from Fox Muzak outlets. Even as Texas descends into gross asininity and willful delusion, Fox Muzak viewers never tremble at the unexpected lurches toward hate and bigotry or feel their stomachs drop during freefalls regarding standards of decency and conscience—i.e., *if brown children are held in cages at our border, they deserve to be . . . if young women can't keep their legs together, they don't deserve sovereignty over their own bodies or complete access to reproductive choices . . . and if desperate immigrants show up in our proud, unrepentantly conservative backwater, we'll ship them up north to Yankee states!*

Fox Muzak consumers get soothing, reassuring conservative elevator prattle on a 24/7 loop. It's calming background noise, and its consumers absorb the same ceaseless, prescribed codifiers.

> *Honor. Liberty. Forefathers.*
> *United. Freedom. God.*
> *Hard Work. Duty. Patriot.*

Fox Muzak personalities do occasionally lapse into sets of hostile jargon, but it almost invariably serves to affirm their prescribed positive codifiers.

> *Science. Academics. Abortion.*
> *Rapers. Murderers. Sex ring.*
> *Socialist. Liberal. Traitor.*

It may barely register at first, but repeating is believing.

It's the cadence of denial and resignation, passed along as practical faith and prudent judgment. It's the language of superficiality and hatred, but spoon-fed like Gerber baby food to generations of feckless Boomers, Gen-X rubes, and Millennial waifs so they don't have to rage, rage against the dying of the light or even be alarmed by the accelerating descent of our nation's formerly celebrated place in the world.

Ever since Fox Muzak landed in Texas, it's owned Texas and governed Texas. And the Democrats here and across America have no real answer for it.

But how could they?

Ailes' GOP TV has half the American population no longer even pretending to believe in American ideals. And the tough questions and honest answers about this stupefying development involve complexity and require nuanced conversations, neither of which the largest percentage of American voters find entertaining or will entertain, much less consider.

And not to be redundant, but how could they?

With the middle class gutted and most working Americans laboring furiously just to stay afloat, who has time for nuance or complexity? Certainly not our employers or our mortgage companies.

Who has time to contemplate the novelty and wisdom of America's great experiment or what's written at the base of the Statue of Liberty?

How many Americans still wonder at the incredible audacity of the New World concept of due process (and how it's still not universally observed) or the courage of a clear mandate of separation of church and state (and how it's now flagrantly ignored)?

From elevators, Muzak tunes spread to grocery stores, shopping centers, airports, cruise ships, corporate offices, and bingo parlors. And psychological studies have shown that Muzak makes listeners more comfortable with being consumers, with buying more, and arguably even buying into things more, in general.

Repetitive, tonal simplicity.

Uplifting, uncomplicated melody.

Honor. Liberty. Forefathers.
United. Freedom. God.
Hard Work. Duty. Patriot.

Not so coincidentally, Muzak is also great for insane asylums, but most sane folks aren't susceptible to it.

Capitalism was a great idea when the United States composed seven percent of the world population but somehow consumed two-thirds of the planet's natural resources, but now unrestrained, unregulated capitalism is global, and resources are scarce and human beings are consuming 1.7 times more than the planet can produce. It's become an unsustainable social cancer destroying our own habitat and extinguishing whole species wholesale. Our children will rarely consume foodstuffs pollenated by real bees. GMOs will fill the gaping holes in our food supply chain with unwholesome substitutes. Our children will not enjoy fair pensions or natural longevity. Social Darwinism, arranged in hierarchies determined by wealth, will reign triumphant and be enforced in dooming perpetuity. And our children and our children's children—especially here in Texas—will never be taught what things were really like before. The truth. The truth about what happened. The truth about what's happening. And why plenty of us are mad enough to spit.

We have been reckless and unwise. And the repercussions are already being felt.

Critical Human Race Theory is even more dangerous and undesirable than Critical Race Theory.

Because they hate us for our freedom.
Because Big Oil.
Because unrestrained, unregulated capitalism.
Because uninformed, unconscionable American Empire.

Though occasionally tempered with the cautionary prejudices of the meek, GOP TV offers lie-affirming daydreams and the deluded slumber of the pseudo-just. Challenging or even cluttering these lie-affirming daydreams or creating unrest is honest and noble but a losing proposition. Attempting or even talking about attempting to disentangle us from our existing and rapidly worsening existential nightmares is political suicide.

Progressive leadership is mostly guilty of telling us too much of what we don't want to hear. It slaps our wrists for past and present mistakes and asks that we atone for our existential indiscretions and social transgressions before it's too late.

Then Fox Muzak swoops in, feigns indignance, and tells us exactly what we want to hear while it holds our hands and pats our heads.

Ailes was clear from the beginning. GOP TV doesn't require you to think. GOP TV doesn't want you to think.

But at least the right's liftmen are managing our plummet with comforting, profitable fortitude.

Say Their Names

October 7, 2021

I watched Jordan Peele's *Candyman*[39] the other night, and it freaked me out.

Especially as a Texan.

Can acts of injustice curse a place? Can acts of monstrosity—as Peele (et al) suggest—stain a community?

A quasi-sequel to the 1992 film of the same name, *Candyman* explores the affirmative answer to these questions. And that's what scares me.

Over the last several years, I've researched and written about numerous acts of injustice and monstrosity in Texas. And, no, "monstrosity" is not too strong a word. In 2014, The History Press published my second book. *The 1910 Slocum Massacre: An Act of Genocide in East Texas* explored the history behind a wholesale slaughter of African Americans that occurred just south of Palestine, Texas, in the early 20th century. The number of casualties far exceeded those of the Rosewood Massacre in Florida in 1923 and rivaled those of the Tulsa Race Massacre in 1921. And hardly anyone in Texas had ever even heard of it.

In 2015, I followed up the Slocum Massacre book with *Black Holocaust: The Paris Horror and a Legacy of Texas Terror*, released by Eakin Press. The term "holocaust" was too

The burning at the stake of Henry Hillard in Tyler, Texas in 1895. *Public domain.*

strong for my first publisher, and probably too controversial in general, but I felt I owed it to the subject matter. Between 1861 and 1933, more than forty Black men were burned at the stake in Texas. And not like the witches who were said to have been burned at the stake in Salem, Massachusetts—because that never happened—but like real, living, breathing human beings—and fellow Texans—being burned at the stake, often in front of cheering white folks.

Cheering. White. Folks.

Before *Friday Night Lights*, the big game was barbecues on the courthouse lawn.

Four black men were burned at the stake in the Paris area, three in Sulphur Springs, three in Kirven, two in Waco, at least two in in Tyler,[40] one in Rockwall, one in Hillsboro, one in Temple, one in Belton, one in Conroe, one in Sherman, one in Texarkana, one in Corsicana, one in Greenville, and so on. And some of these cases involved levels of evil and depravity that make the *Candyman* plotlines pale (pardon the pun) in comparison.

In Paris in 1893, a mob of thousands watched on as Henry Smith—a Black man suspected of raping and killing a white toddler—was tortured with red hot iron pokers for 45 minutes (by the infant's father and older brother) before being gruesomely burned to a crisp. They peeled away the skin on his arms, legs, back, and abdomen by rolling the searing pokers on contact, reheating them as necessary, and then used them to boil away his eyeballs and burn out his tongue. The white crowd cheered the vicious cruelty and raucously jeered the Black suspect's moans of pain and suffering. The Paris mayor even canceled school for the day so the community's children could view the spectacle with their parents.

In 1895, the citizens of Tyler denied Henry Hillard—a Black man suspected of raping and killing a white woman—due process and burned him at the stake in front a mob of thousands, partially extinguishing and then reviving the flames so as to extend the effect and general excruciation of the torture to entertain and appease white onlookers. After futilely begging his tormentors to put him out of his misery,

Lynching of Jesse Washington in Waco, Texas on May 15, 1916. *Public domain.*

Hillard began attempting to bash his own brains out by slamming the back of his head against the iron rail he was affixed to.

In 1915, the citizens of Waco witnessed the ghastly burning at the stake of Jesse Washington, a mentally handicapped Black man suspected of killing a white woman, in full view of the mayor and the local police. The perpetrating mob castrated Washington on the way to the stake and also cut off his fingers. Then, after several times being raised and lowered into the flames for the greatest effect as he was burned alive, Washington began trying to escape his hellish fate by climbing the chain with fingerless hands.

And these are just a fraction of the dozens of macabre atrocities that make the origins of *Candyman* seem tame. Texans, our forebears, committed atrocities in front of cheering white neighbors. And then created lynching postcards and stereographic viewing sets to celebrate and commemorate these horrific events, which—*don't kid yourself*—many of our great-great-great grandads and kinfolk jovially referred to as "roasts" and, I repeat, "barbecues."

Mr. Peele and his associates, and their predecessors, touch on something fundamentally raw here,   something largely

"A rare horror film that has something to say." The remake may be even better. *Image from* Philadelphia Inquirer *archives.*

unheralded and involving injuries long concealed and clearly unhealed.

I'd urge fellow Texans to refrain from the namesake character's game, because the facts in Texas are darker than the fiction in *Candyman*.

That's why conservatives don't want the truth taught in schools.

Red Wrong

March 4, 2022

If you were the average, red-blooded, teenaged American boy in the late '80s, you weren't sure of too many things, if anything at all, but on one issue there was no tentativeness and no serious debate. The Russians sucked. The Russkies were definitely and unequivocally the bad guys.

Rambo told us so in *Rocky IV* (1985). Rocky told us so in *Rambo III* (1988). Tom Cruise said so in *Top Gun* (1986). And well before Sylvester Stallone and Cruise told us so, Ponyboy Curtis (C. Thomas Howell in the 1983 film *The Outsiders*, starring alongside yet to be famous Cruise and *Platoon* cherry Charlie Sheen), Texas boy Patrick Swayze (also in *The Outsiders*, and *Dirty Dancing* in 1987, *Road House* in 1989, and more), and older Texas boy Powers Boothe—and Charlie Sheen all told us so in the surprise blockbuster of 1984: *Red Dawn*

One reviewer described *Red Dawn* as "a self-congratulatory little B-picture, the sort America does so well." Set in the build-up to WWIII, it is "a loving chronicle of juvenile heroism in Russian-occupied Colorado"—which, yes, sounds absolutely preposterous. But bear with me.

One thing this pre-"woke" action flick gets right is letting schoolboys and schoolgirls take up arms—both Lea

Richard Crenna and Sylvester Stallone in *Rambo III*, which "revises *Rambo II*'s rewrite of Vietnam".[41] This is humorous because Sly dodged the Vietnam draft by attending the American College of Switzerland in Leysin. *Image from* Daily News Leader *archives.*

Thompson, who later played Marty McFly's mom and girlfriend in the 1985 mega-blockbuster *Back to the Future*, and Jennifer Grey, Swayze's yet-to-be-famous tango partner "Baby" in the sappy, happy mega-blockbuster *Dirty Dancing*, perform feisty female combatant roles. All the children "caught behind enemy lines become crack guerillas overnight," the critic goes on, and "slaughter nobly" and "die even more so." At the time *Red Dawn* was released, it was considered one of the most violent films ever made by the *Guinness Book of World Records* and the National Coalition on Television Violence, because it featured 134 acts of violence per hour, or 2.23 acts per minute. As Todd Snider, my old college rugby teammate-turned-folk singer likes to say, "In America, we like our bad guys dead . . . It's called box office, baby."

That kind of box office revenue (though it made Stallone and Cruise untold millions), however, contributes to a boxed-in or tunnel-visioned view of the world. *Red Dawn* stretched our red, white, and blue underwear into rabidly patriotic salutes, and this staunch patriotism fortified our political views and remained surprisingly potent in our minds, even as we became less potent between the sheets.

Then, Trumpism walked by in a red, white, and blue—but mostly white—bikini, and suddenly (and somewhat insanely) legions of Gen X men and seemingly most of their elders were reminded of those unchallenged, seemingly unassailable red, white, and blue underwear tents of yesteryear. Which was good or bad, depending on your susceptibility or naivete in general.

But now, a real *Red Dawn* is happening in Ukraine, and the voters, pundits, and politicians who offered standing salutes to Herr Trump's friendship and admiration for Comrade Putin are soberly decrying the dictator's actions but remaining silent on their complicity in the entire debacle. Their Orange Messiah is commending Putin's invasion of Ukraine, but his devoted conservative and Republican supporters are carefully compartmentalizing his comments, already separating the myth from the man and thereby self-censoring Critical Russia Theory to avoid contemplating their own culpability or face serious self-examination.

The same folks who had boners for the original *Red Dawn* and its gratuitously violent plotline—which followed them into their fifties—have conveniently gone limp in terms of

Charlie Sheen and Texan Patrick Swayze in the surprise 1984 blockbuster, *Red Dawn. Courtesy of* The Age.

memory, responsibility, and existential honesty, because it calls into question their votes, their worldview, and their fearless leader's shit-stained, red silk boxers. Back then, these 'Muricans screamed, "Wolverines!" every time they orgasmed (with or without their girlfriends), but now that the Russians are really invading and slaughtering real Outsiders, real Rambos, real Ponyboys, and genuine dirty-dancing Babys indiscriminately, American conservatives are grudgingly but quietly admitting their mistake or ignoring the whole thing.

How does that feel?

Is the worst thing about being an American conservative or Republican these days having a conscience or being forced to pretend you don't have one?

Or having to forget you were young once?

The headlines out of Ukraine are straight from the *Red Dawn* plotline, and we're seeing the movie again, except for real this time—but, instead of aligning himself with the Ukrainian freedom fighters, the MAGA faithful's Orange Messiah was and is aligned with the bad guys from the '80s. And now a vast majority of *reTrumplicans* can't admit they were wrong.

Dead wrong.

Red wrong.

Pigmentation in Conroe

A good friend emailed me a couple weeks back and asked me why Donald Trump had recently spoke in Conroe, Texas.

I didn't know. I hadn't known Trump was even visiting Texas. I haven't been watching the news a lot lately.

I emailed her back: "No. Probably a motivated gaggle of his fans there. It's also, of course, a place where they burned a Black man at the stake."

Hmmm, I mumbled to myself.

Then my mind began sifting through past research. Dates, places, faces, events—images. What year was that, I wondered.

I looked it up. And I looked up the 2020 presidential election results.

Conroe is in Montgomery County, north of Harris County, where Houston sits. In the election, Biden won Harris with 56% of the votes. Trump was victorious in Montgomery with 71%.

Was it a coincidence? Was my friend, who believes in "alignments," especially in relation to causation, nudging me?

Was it happenstance that a community where an innocent young Black man named Joe Winters was burned at the stake—on the courthouse square, no less, for being in a relationship with a young white woman—might endorse, support, or host Donald J. Trump on his "Save America Tour"? Was it coincidence that former President Trump appeared in Conroe just a few months shy of the 100th anniversary of Winters' hellish execution?

An association—even a strong one—is not a proof of causation, but research in terms of correlation was called for. For the uninitiated, I am the author of *The 1910 Slocum Massacre: An Act of Genocide in East Texas* (History Press 2014). The book was influential in some ways, including the placement of a historical marker commemorating the atrocity, but my follow-up, *Black Holocaust: The Paris Horror and a Legacy of Texas Terror* (Eakin Press 2015), hardly moved the dial at all. Even in the Black community. Perhaps because it was too much, too dark, too terrible to consider, much less process. Michael Hurd,[42] a native Houstonian and director of the Texas Black History Preservation Project (TBHPP) at the time who is currently serving as director of Prairie View A&M's Texas Institute for the Preservation of History and Culture (which is digitally documenting 500 years of Black history in Texas) admitted as much. TBHPP lauded the Slocum Massacre account but was cold on the *Black Holocaust* book. Hurd told me he just couldn't read it, that he couldn't bear to read it.

I understood. I truly and sincerely understood.

My *Black Holocaust* book chronicled white terrorism and white monstrosity on a level and scale that's still hard to contemplate, much less fully grasp the implications of. For Blacks or whites.

Nothing happens in a vacuum.

Image of Joe Winters being burned at the stake in Conroe, Texas on May 20, 1922. *From the November 1922 edition of the NAACP's* Crisis *magazine.*

Trump was welcomed in Conroe the same way he would be welcomed in other Texas cities like Waco, Tyler, Paris, Sulphur Springs, Greenville, Hillsboro, Rockwall, Corsicana, or Sherman, and maybe Belton and Temple. The late 19th- or early 20th-century citizens of these communities all burned a Black man at the stake, a Black man who was usually innocent. And the citizens of Waco, Tyler, Paris, and Sulphur Springs burned more than one innocent Black man at the stake.

But I digress. I mentioned correlation.

In the 2020 presidential election, 52% of Texas voters voted for the incumbent. In Bell County, which includes Temple and Belton but also gets closer to progressive Travis County and Austin (where Trump received only 28% of the vote), Trump garnered 53% of the electorate. In Chip and Joanna Gaines County—I'm sorry, I mean McLennan County—whose county seat is Waco, Trump received 61% of the vote. In

Navarro County (county seat Corsicana), Trump prevailed with 63% of the ballots. In Rockwall County (county seat Rockwall, just east of Dallas), voters—whose forebears, like Conroe's, burned an innocent young Black man at the stake for courting a young white woman—went 68% for Trump. Montgomery County (again, county seat Conroe)—where an innocent Black man was burned at the stake 100 years ago this year—Trump got 71% of the vote. Grayson County (county seat Sherman) went for Trump-Pence 74%. Hopkins County (county seat Sulphur Springs) gave Trump the nod with 76% of ballots cast. Lamar County, where four Black men were burned at the stake in or near Paris, went for a MAGA sequel at a clip of 78%, and in Hill County (county seat Hillsboro)—where an intellectually disabled Black man was burned on the courthouse square in 1919—constituents cast 80% of their ballots for Trump.

Anecdotal?

Possibly. Arguably.

But in Cooke County (county seat Gainesville)—home of The Great Hanging[43]—Trump also prevailed with almost 80% of the vote. And even Anderson County, where the 1910 Slocum Massacre started, managed a Red State-respectable 74% of the ballots. And then there's Comanche County, where a Black man was lynched in 1886 and all the Black residents of the entire county were expelled, and the small town of De Leon infamously posted a sign that said, "Nigger, don't let the sun go down on you in this town," the Trump-Pence ticket was in like Flynn, boasting over 83% of the electorate.

Causation can be immediate, but it is often incremental, long-lasting, and repercussive. As of the 2000 Census, for one instance, the demographics of Comanche County included a Black population of only 0.44%. For another, historically racist counties not-so-coincidentally and almost invariably prefer Trump and/or conservative leadership, and, of course, rural communities with less diversity and less educational opportunities prefer Trump and/or conservative leadership.

Does anybody really believe that the fact that Texas conservatives find Critical Race Theory anathema is mere coincidence? Is the fact that Texas Republicans are trying to limit voting rights and political representation (via gerrymandering) for persons of color simply happenstance?

The numbers don't lie.

The history doesn't lie.

And the sad, sickening irony of it all is the image of Donald Trump standing at a Conroe podium and saying, "If I run, and if I win, we will treat those people from [the] January 6th [2021 insurrection[44]] fairly … and if it requires pardons, we will give them pardons because they are being treated so unfairly."

Wow. That's exactly how the faithful white conservatives of Conroe felt about the perpetrators of the ghastly execution of Joe Winters 100 years ago. None of them were even arrested or charged.

Their pigmentation was their pardon.

The Party of "Abortion" in Texas

June 2, 2021[45]

It's ironic that Texas Republicans are so committed to abolishing abortion.

Abortion is their primary modus operandi.[46]

Abortion is basically their chief reason for being.

Every election season, Republicans try to abort voting rights, especially for Texans of a different complexion. And for as much weeping and gnashing of teeth that Republicans do about late-term abortion, they would gleefully abort the results of the last presidential election. An inordinate number of Texas Republicans tried on January 6. They can't help themselves.

While the United States of America was established by the descendants of immigrants, the Republic of Texas was largely founded by actual immigrants. The only two native Texans who signed the Texas Declaration of Independence were Jose Francisco Ruiz and Jose Antonio Navarro, so besides the original founders without Spanish surnames, Republicans are fierce opponents of immigration and naturalization. Republicans would abort immigration altogether if they could, but in recent years, they've had to settle for separating immigrant children from their parents and placing them in cages along our border. It's sad, but at least the victims are brown.

Pro-choice protester making a salient point outside the U.S. Supreme Court in 2016. *Wikipedia Commons.*

Texas Republicans aren't real keen on persons of color in general—immigrant or no—unless they're carrying a football, which brings to mind another white conservative conundrum. It's difficult for Texas Republicans to think highly of themselves and their forebears if the facts about Texas independence and the countless atrocities committed against persons of color are widely propagated. Truth-telling, therefore, must be aborted.[47] It's a constant priority. But—to their tremendous benefit—the only thing more powerful than white fragility in Texas these days is conservative white political agility.

When Texas Republicans aren't obsessing over ways to disenfranchise persons of color, they go after women. Texas Republicans have a perpetual Viagra-charged hard-on for aborting women's reproductive rights and also fight against fair pay for Texas women. It's no wonder there are fewer and fewer Republican babies around.

And there's the real rub.

White women have the most abortions. If women of color were the largest demographic utilizing birth control or terminating their pregnancies, Texas Republicans would make birth control and abortion kits available at every Whataburger drive-thru in the state.

I'm not trying to be funny. There's no reason to mince words. Their record is clear.

Texas Republicans initially aborted the insurance exchange clause of Obamacare to poison the proverbial well. It denied millions of folks affordable health care and, ultimately, killed Texans just to score political points. More recently, Texas Republicans aborted the right to protest Big Oil and regularly abort clean air and water measures, poisoning millions of Texans, destroying animal habitats, and restricting access to precious natural resources. And Texas Republicans are currently working to abort reasonable gun control efforts, abort real reforms of the Texas power grid (which killed dozens of Texans during the ice storm in February), and abort the homeless (instead of mitigating the conditions that create them).

Oh, and they get away with all this because the Fairness Doctrine[48] was aborted back in 1987, ushering in a media environment where a propaganda machine like Fox News can brainwash conservative voters, convincing them to self-abort theretofore long-standing notions of honesty, conscience, and human decency.

In a word, Texas Republicans are more of a miscarriage than an abortion—of justice, of intellect, of forethought, and of reasonable governance, but abortion is the means by which they simultaneously make Texas a laughingstock and a menace.

Adulthood's End

January 17, 2024 (as "Kiddie Table")

When I think too long on contemporary grown-ups, I do not like what I see.

Something about it reminds of Charles Foster Kane's (Orson Welles) final scene in *Citizen Kane*, after his love interest decides to leave him. He begins throwing luggage around and tearing up her room, and then, winded by the effort, spots a small snow globe and picks it up. The artificial snow begins swirling around the translucent sphere, and Kane is taken aback—and back—to a time when he was a child.

His famous final line is, "Rosebud".

After he dies, a large gathering of the rest of the cast wonder what his last word meant.

Welles, himself, said it best. "Rosebud is the trade name of a cheap, little sled on which Kane was playing on the day he was taken away from his home and his mother. In his subconsciousness, it represented the simplicity, the comfort and, above all, the lack of responsibility in his home, and it also stood for his mother's love, which Kane never lost."

The devolution of modern adults is a collective treatise on nostalgic longing, but often not for experiences we ever really had or adventures we even partook in. Most of us didn't have sleds. Most of us didn't have mothers waiting for us at home— they were working. But we had TV, sports or video games. And, after a while, we had sports on TV or played sports-themed video games. Or skipped sports altogether and focused on fantasy-themed video games, never actually experiencing thrill of riding or navigating a snow sled, cheap or otherwise.

A "Beavis" (of *Beavis and Butthead*[49]) cosplayer at the 2015 Phoenix Comicon. Beavis was an early *cornholer*, presenting himself here as "The Great Cornholio."

Like so many things in contemporary human existence, it is not so much a lost art as the vanishing knowledge of physically inhabited moments that define life at an elemental level.

If *Citizen Kane* is ever remade, "Rosebud" may refer to an Atari joystick. Or it may never need to be remade because many adults remain committed to video games into their fifties. And many are consumed by sports viewing or sports wagering, even if they never played the sports they watch or wager on. Many grown men and women are consumed by fantasy, video games, anime, cosplay, or plain old childhood nostalgia. You can find pacifiers for adults and baby wipes for "dudes". There are now official, adult dodgeball leagues and shuffleboard, horseshoes and croquet have all been replaced the most childish joke of them all, cornhole. Which is particularly inane, because "cornhole" is sexual slang for an anus. The term reportedly came into use as a noun in early Twentieth century America due to the use of dry corn cobs in lieu of toilet paper. Its verb form was popularized in the 1930's as slang for engaging in anal sex. It's a potty punchline on steroids.

And as adulthood ends, childhood teases a lifetime appointment. Children today spend more time on their phone than they do outside. Physically playing less, and, as they become teenagers, having less sex. And this, while—not to put too fine (or, as it were, coarse) a point on it, their parents are shaving away their pubic hair so that their genitals look more like their children's. Which seems doubly asinine, because, for most of human existence, the appearance of pubic hair historically announced a child's approach to biological adulthood.

In fact—though it's nothing new, just accelerated and increasingly universal—adults are spending billions if not trillions of dollars a year to appear as little aged or adult as possible. And it demonstrates a dangerous, burgeoning communal neurosis that is characterized by a headlong flight into infantilism that modern society clearly fosters if not encourages. Meanwhile, their idle child counterparts are endeavoring mightily to avoid adult endeavors.

English poet William Wordsworth wrote "the child is the father to man" in 1802, and maybe it was true 220 years ago. But today more and more men and women are perpetually infantile and their children are trapped in an infantile stasis. It's all play-pretend and we are each encouraged to "live our own truth." With or without one another or the last or next generation. One of the next fortunes will probably be made by the creator of adult bed mobiles featuring spinning *Game of Thrones* or *Star Wars* figures, to sooth us when we silence the iPhone or turn off the flatscreen TV and try to fall asleep.

But back to the kids.

Social media and digital communication platforms allow youths to forego interpersonal, face-to-face engagements, so young people are less and less capable of navigating them healthily or productively. Many young people are more committed and devoted to virtual relationships than actual, face-to-face connections with the people they live amongst or encounter every day. Their personal detachment leads to impractical isolation and retards their social development.

There is certainly more to life than work, but consider this passage regarding infantilism in the workplace by Valentin Tikhonov in *Medium* earlier this year:

> *Employers need employees who are self-motivated, able to take initiative, and willing to learn and adapt. When adults exhibit childlike behavior, such as expecting constant praise and recognition, avoiding challenges, and being unable to handle criticism, they become a liability rather than an asset to their employer. This can lead to decreased productivity, increased turnover, and a general decline in the quality of work being produced.*

Sound familiar?

Frenchman Alexis de Tocqueville would famously observe "enlightened self-interest" in America during his travels in the 19th century. He noted that Americans voluntarily join together in associations to further the interests of the group and, thereby, to serve their own interests.[50] It clearly didn't last.

Well, not if you avoid the work force.

But it's as true in in human relationships as it is in the workplace.

It's true of our 46th president.

It defines our political parties.

It's inherent in contemporary social movements. It often even seems true of Americans as a whole, because we are no longer conjointly whole. Free market Capitalism has converted de Toqueville's chronicle of "enlightened self-interest" to simply self-interest. And our exaggeratedly innocent and uncomplicated past—where we had less opinions and enjoyed less responsibilities—beckons almost dreamlike, an attractive mirage.

Want the honest truth?

The real reason the old want their youth back so badly (or never want to leave it) is because they didn't spend it particularly productively and didn't appreciate it for what it was at the time. And, ultimately, they have this simultaneously in common with Gen Z, which, excepting a lack of pubic hair, is literally doing and experiencing even less than their parental or grandparental units.

We're no longer encouraged to be grown-ups or adults—which allows the powers that be to manipulate and pit us against each other more easily while they bury us all under their own childlike indulgences.

Which means our children's "Rosebud" will be an earbud and their children's children will likely enjoy implanted earbuds to feed them the answers and teach them what to believe—*but now how to think*—rendering them children even as adults.

We Don't Deserve Another Planet

I'm scared. I worry a lot.

I'm afraid for our future. I'm afraid for our species.

I'm afraid *of* our species.

Homo Sapiens corrupt or foul any ecosystem that lies in the path of their economic interests. *Homo Sapiens* marginalize and/or exterminate almost every species of fellow inhabitant that it comes into contact with. *Homo Sapiens* are defiling the gasping blue orb they call home, but they press on almost entirely heedless of their loathsome wrongheadedness.

You, me and every human being up and down our street, across the nation and throughout the world, en masse, comprise a sinister planetary menace. It is not our intent; we just can't or won't control ourselves.

Fort Worth writer and former resident John Graves once said that human beings would be finished when they stopped "understanding the old pull toward green things and living things." But we're already there. We are monstrously out of sync with the natural world. We no longer even take part in the most basic facets of our own sustenance.

Technology has replaced survival processes with leisure. Our livelihoods are based on ancillary subsistence modes which translate into to petty barter for factory farming and mechanized industrial slaughter. We live on pre-processed pseudo-nourishment. We reside in prefabricated shelters

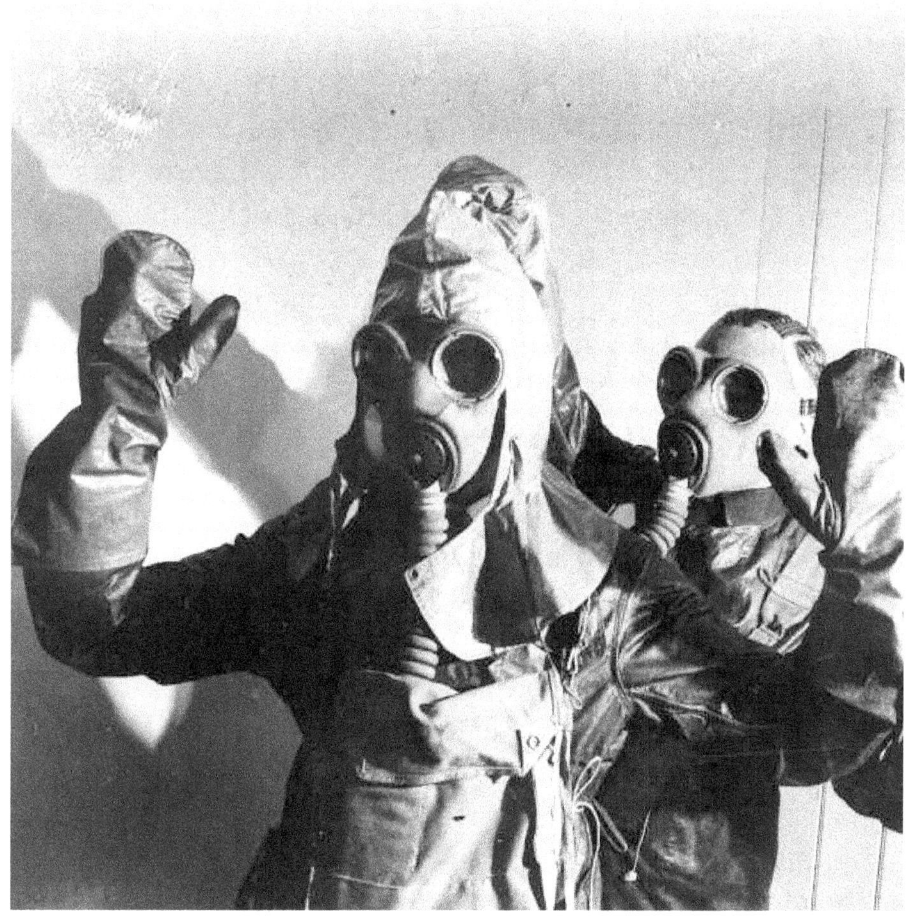

We'll just have to adapt. *Wikipedia Commons.*[51]

bathed in artificial light and filled with conditioned air. We don't thrive as vital, fully-functional creatures; we merely exist as detached bystanders.

In our natural state we were never idle or bored or prone to weight gains due to a sedentary lifestyle. We were constantly involved in the means of survival, hands-on, acute and in-tune. We didn't need Vegas or roller coasters or Viagra. Every day was a gamble and every food-source capture or kill was a victory if not an outright adrenaline rush. In our present state we struggle to survive business as usual with any useful, natural instincts intact.

Several seconds before the late August 2011 earthquake near the National Zoo in DC, flamingos grouped together, upper mammals climbed trees and lemurs sounded alarm calls. In our early existence, we probably weren't much different than the spooked animals at the National Zoo. We probably sensed phenomena like earthquakes at an elemental level, before they happened, because we were more in touch with our habitat. Truth be told, we arguably knew more then as preyed-upon primitives than we know now as reckless louts at the top of the food chain.

We are a species run amok, obtuse and self-destructive. It's time to debate Capitalism in a world of limited resources; it's time to have a referendum on unaccountable Technology. If the swift-shod proliferation of excessive consumption in the name of ever-increasing profit margins reduces humanity to a lethal scourge, Capitalism is an evil that can no longer be tolerated. If the unavoidable byproducts of technology are human overpopulation, the pollution or contamination of our air, water and food supplies, biological exploitation and artificial preservation—all created at the expense of the planet and our fellow species—technology is an evil that can no longer be promoted. If Capitalism and technology cannot be practiced with conscience, then we cannot conscientiously engage in them.

These issues warrant debate in the fore of this historical moment because humankind is toying with the notion of exploring and/or colonizing other earth-like planets in their galactic vicinity. It's one thing for us to plunder and savage our own home. It's quite another to destroy someone else's home.

We must stop averting our eyes. We need to quit ignoring our crimes. In the grand scheme of things we've become a vicious virus that should be isolated and confined, allowing our madness to run its course, come what may.

As bad as things stand on Earth for inhabitants other than *Homo Sapiens*, at least *Homo Sapiens* are contained here. And the fledgling life-support and propulsion technologies that keep us from exploring deep-space ensure our quarantine.

If we perish, our perilous, suicidal propensities should die with us and not be flung amongst the galaxies to infect or endanger other living systems. The species *Homo Sapiens* had its chance.

Tragically, we're wasting it.

ABOUT THE AUTHOR

E. R. Bills is an award-winning author and freelance journalist. His works include *Texas Obscurities: Stories of the Peculiar, Exceptional and Nefarious* (2013), *The 1910 Slocum Massacre: An Act of Genocide in East Texas* (2014), *Black Holocaust: The Paris Horror and a Legacy of Texas Terror* (2015), *Texas Far and Wide: The Tornado with Eyes, Gettysburg's Last Casualty, the Celestial Skipping Stone and Other Tales* (History Press 2017), *The San Marcos 10: An Anti-War Protest in Texas* (2019), *Texas Oblivion: Mysterious Disappearances, Escapes and Cover-Ups* (2021), *Fear and Loathing in the Lone Star State* (2021), *100 Things to Do in Texas Before You Die* (2022) and *Tell-Tale Texas: Investigations into Infamous History* (2023).

Bills has also written for the *Austin American-Statesman*, the *Fort Worth Star-Telegram*, *Texas Co-Op Power* magazine, *Fort Worth Magazine* and *Fort Worth Weekly*. He currently resides in North Texas.

APPENDIX I

The Inconvenient Truth
by Patrick Crusius

About Me

In general, I support the Christchurch shooter and his manifesto.[52] This attack is a response to the Hispanic invasion of Texas. They are the instigators, not me. I am simply defending my country from cultural and ethnic replacement brought on by an invasion. Some people will think this statement is hypocritical because of the nearly complete ethnic and cultural destruction brought to the Native Americans by our European ancestors, but this just reinforces my point. The natives didn't take the invasion of Europeans seriously, and now what's left is just a shadow of what was. My motives for this attack are not at all personal. Actually the Hispanic community was not my target before I read *The Great Replacement*.[53] This manifesto will cover the political and economic reasons behind the attack, my gear, my expectations of what response this will generate and my personal motivations and thoughts.

Political Reasons

In short, America is rotting from the inside out, and peaceful means to stop this seem to be nearly impossible. The inconvenient truth is that our leaders, both Democrat AND Republican, have been failing us for decades. They are either complacent or involved in one of the biggest betrayals of the American public in our history. The takeover of the United States government by unchecked corporations. I could write a ten page essay on all the damage these corporations have caused, but here is what is important. Due to the death of the baby boomers, the increasingly anti-immigrant rhetoric of the right and the ever increasing Hispanic population, America will soon become a one party-state. The Democrat party will own America and they know it. They have already begun the transition by pandering heavily to the Hispanic voting bloc in the 1st Democratic Debate. They intend to use open borders, free healthcare for illegals, citizenship and more to enact a political coup by importing and then legalizing millions of new voters. With policies like these, the Hispanic support for Democrats will likely become nearly unanimous in the future. The heavy Hispanic population in Texas will make us a Democrat stronghold. Losing Texas and a few other states with heavy Hispanic population to the Democrats is all it would take for them to win nearly every presidential election. Although the Republican Party is also terrible. Many factions within the Republican Party are pro-corporation. Procorporation pro-immigration. But some factions within the Republican Party don't prioritize corporations over our future. So the Democrats are nearly unanimous with their support of immigration while the Republicans are divided over it. At least with Republicans, the process of mass immigration and citizenship can be greatly reduced.

Economic Reasons

In short, immigration can only be detrimental to the future of America. Continued immigration will make one of the biggest issues of our time, automation, so much worse. Some sources say that in under two decades, half of American jobs will be lost to it. Of course some people will be retrained, but most will not. So it makes no sense to keep on letting millions of illegal or legal immigrants flood into the United States, and to keep the tens of millions that are already here. Invaders who also have close to the highest birthrate of all ethnicities in America. In the near future, America will have to initiate a basic universal income to prevent widespread poverty and civil unrest as people lose their jobs. Joblessness in itself is a source of civil unrest. The less dependents on a government welfare system, the better. The lower the unemployment rate, the better. Achieving ambitious social projects like universal healthcare and UBI would be far more likely to succeed if tens of millions of dependents are removed.

Even though new migrants do the dirty work, their kids typically don't. They want to live the American Dream which is why they get college degrees and fill higher-paying skilled positions. This is why corporations lobby for even more illegal immigration even after decades of it happening. They need to keep replenishing the low-skilled labor pool. Even as migrant children flood skilled jobs, Corporations make this worse by lobbying for even more work visas to be issued for skilled foreign workers to come here. Recently, the senate under a REPUBLICAN administration has greatly increased the number of foreign works that will take American jobs. Remember that both Democrats and Republicans support immigration and work visas. Corporations need to keep replenishing the labor pool for both skilled and unskilled jobs to keep wages down. So Automation is a good thing as it will eliminate the need for new migrants to fill unskilled jobs. Jobs that Americans can't survive on anyway. Automation can and would replace millions of low-skilled jobs if immigrants were deported. This source of competition for skilled labor from immigrants and visa holders around the world has made a very difficult situation even worse for natives as they compete in the skilled job market. To compete, people have to get better credentials by spending more time in college. It used to be that a high school degree was worth something. Now a bachelor's degree is what's recommended to be competitive in the job market. The cost of college degrees has exploded as they value has plummeted. This has led to a generation of indebted, overqualified students filling menial, low paying and unfulfilling jobs. Of course these migrants and their children have contributed to the problem, but are not the sole cause of it.

The American lifestyle affords our citizens an incredible quality of life. However, our lifestyle is destroying the environment of our country. The decimation of the environment is creating a massive burden for future generations. Corporations are heading the destruction of our environment by shamelessly overharvesting resources. This has been a problem for decades. For example, this phenomenon is brilliantly portrayed in the decades old classic "The Lorax." Water sheds around the country, especially in agricultural areas, are being depleted. Fresh water is being polluted from farming and oil drilling operations. Consumer culture is creating thousands of tons of unnecessary plastic waster and electronic waste, and recycling to help slow this down is almost non-existent. Urban sprawl creates inefficient cities which unnecessarily destroys millions of acres of land. We even use god knows how many trees worth of paper towels just to wipe water off our hands. Everything I have seen and heard in my short life has led me to believe that the average American isn't willing to change their lifestyle, even if the changes only cause a slight inconvenience. The government is unwilling to tackle these issues beyond empty promises since they are owned by corporations. Corporations that also like immigration because more people means a bigger market for their products. I just want to say that I love the people of this country, but god damn most of y'all are just too stubborn to change your lifestyle. So the next logical step is to decrease the number of people in America using resources. If we can get rid of enough people, then our way of life can become more sustainable.

Gear

Main gun: AK47 (WASR 10) – I realized pretty quickly that this isn't a great choice since it's the civilian version of the ak47. It's not designed to shoot rounds quickly, so it overheats massively after about 100 shots fired in quick succession. I'll have to use a heat-resistant glove to get around this.

8m3 bullet: This bullet, unlike pretty much any other 7.62x39 bullet, actually fragments like a postol hollow point when shot out of an ak47 at the cost of penetration. Penetration is still reasonable, but not nearly as high as a normal ak47 bullet. The ak47 is definitely a bad choice without this bullet design, and may still be with it.

Other gun (if I get one): Ar15 – pretty much any variation of this gun doesn't heat up nearly as fast as the AK47. The round of this gun isn't designed to fragment, but instead tumbles inside a target causing lethal wounding. This gun is probably better, but I wanted to explore different options. The ar15 is probably the best gun for military applications but this isn't a military application.

This will be a test of which is more lethal, either it's fragmentation or tumbling.

I didn't spend much time at all preparing for this attack. Maybe a month, probably less. I have to do this before I lose my never. I figured that an under-prepared attack and a manifesto is better than no attack and no manifesto.

Reaction

Statistically, millions of migrants have returned to their home countries to reunite with the family they lost contact with when they moved to America. They come here as economic immigrants, not for asylum reasons. This is an encouraging sign that the Hispanic population is willing to return to their home countries if given the right incentive. An incentive that myself and many other patriotic Americans will provide. This will remove the threat of the Hispanic voting bloc which will make up for the loss of millions of baby boomers. This will also make the elites that run corporations realize that it's not in their interest to continue to piss off Americans. Corporate America doesn't need to be destroyed, but just shown that they are on the wrong side of history. That if they don't bend, they will break.

Personal Reasons and Thoughts

My whole life I have been preparing for a future that currently doesn't exist. The job of my dreams will likely be automated. Hispanics will take control of the local and state government of my beloved Texas, changing policy to better suit their needs. They will turn Texas into an instrument of a political coup which will hasten the destruction of our country. The environment is getting worse by the year. If you take nothing else from this document, remember this: INACTION IS A CHOICE. I can no longer bear the shame of inaction knowing that our founding fathers have endowed me with the rights needed to save our country from the brink of destruction. Our European comrades don't have the gun rights needed to repel the millions of invaders that plague their country. They have no choice but to sit by and watch their countries burn.

America can only be destroyed from the inside-out. If our country falls, it will be the fault of traitors. This is why I see my actions as faultless. Because this isn't an act of imperialism but an act of preservation. America is full of hypocrites who will blast my actions as the sole result of racism and hatred of other countries, despite the extensive evidence of all the problems these invaders cause and will cause. People who are hypocrites because they support imperialistic wars that have caused the loss of tens of thousands of American lives and untold numbers of civilian lives. The argument that mass murder is okay when it is state sanctioned is absurd. Our government has killed a whole lot more people for a whole lot less.

Even if other non-immigrant targets would have a greater impact, I can't bring myself to kill my fellow Americans. Even the Americans that seem hell-bent on destroying our country. Even if they are shameless race misers, massive polluters, haters of our collective values, etc. One day they will see error of their ways. Either when American patriots fail to reform our country and it collapses or when we save it. But they will see the error of their ways. I promise y'all that.

I am against race mixing because it destroys genetic diversity and creates identity problems. Also because it's completely unnecessary and selfish. 2nd and 3rd generation Hispanics form interracial unions at much higher rates than average. Yet another reason to send them back. Cultural and racial diversity is largely temporary. Cultural diversity diminishes as stronger and/or more appealing cultures overtake weaker and/or undesirable ones. Racial diversity will disappear as either race missing or genocide will take place. But the idea of deporting or murdering all non-white Americans is horrific. Many have been here at least as long as the whites, and have done as much to build our country. The best solution to this for would be to divide America into a confederacy of territories with at least 1 territory for each race. This physical separation would nearly eliminate race mixing and improve social unity by granting each race self-determination with their respective territory(s).

My death is likely inevitable. If I'm not killed by the police, then I'll probably be gunned down by one of the invaders. Capture in this case is far worse than dying during the shooting because I'll get the death penalty anyway. Worse still is that I would live knowing that my family despises me. This is why I'm not going to surrender even if I run out of ammo. If I'm captured, it will be because I was subdued somehow.

Remember: it is not cowardly to pick low hanging fruit. AKA Don't attack heavily guarded areas to fulfill your super soldier COD fantasy. Attack low security targets. Even though you might out gun a security guard or police man, they likely beat you in armor, training and numbers. Do not throw away your life on an unnecessarily dangerous target. If a target seems to hot, live to fight another day.

My ideology has not changed for several years. My opinions on automation, immigration, and the rest predate Trump and his campaign for president. I am putting this here because some people will blame the President or certain presidential candidates for the attack. This is not the case. I know that the media will probably call me a white supremacist anyway and blame Trump's rhetoric. The media is infamous for fake news. Their reaction to this attack will likely just confirm that.

Many people that think that the fight for America is already lost. They couldn't be more wrong. This is just the beginning of the fight for America and Europe. I am honored to head the fight to reclaim my country from destruction.

ENDNOTES

1 James Byrd, Jr. (May 2, 1949 – June 7, 1998) was an Black man who was murdered by three white men (two of whom were admitted white supremacists) in Jasper, Texas, on June 7, 1998. Shawn Berry, Lawrence Brewer, and John King dragged him for three miles behind a Ford truck along an asphalt road. Byrd, who remained conscious for much of his ordeal, was killed about halfway through the dragging when his body hit the edge of a culvert, severing his right arm and head. His murderers drove on for another 1 ½ miles and then dumped Byrd's torso in front of a Black church.

2 *If It Bleeds* is a collection of four previously unpublished novellas by American writer Stephen King. The stories are titled "Mr. Harrigan's Phone", "The Life of Chuck", "If It Bleeds", and "Rat". It was released on April 28, 2020.

3 Wikipedia Commons: "A riff on Banksy's famous Flower Bomber street art, this image shows a female librarian getting ready to hurl Margaret Atwood's *The Handmaid's Tale*." Author/Artist: Hafuboti.

4 *The Great Brain* is a series of children's books by American author John D. Fitzgerald (February 3, 1906 – May 30, 1988). Set in the small town of Adenville, Utah, between 1896 and 1898, the stories are based on Fitzgerald's childhood experiences. Chronicled by the first-person voice of John Dennis Fitzgerald, the stories mainly center on the escapades of John's mischievous older brother, Tom Dennis Fitzgerald, a.k.a. "The Great Brain".

5 Flannery O'Connor (March 25, 1925 – August 3, 1964) was an American novelist, short story writer and essayist. She wrote two novels and thirty-one short stories, as well as a number of reviews and commentaries.

O'Connor was a Southern writer who often wrote in a sardonic Southern Gothic style and relied heavily on regional settings and grotesque characters, often in violent situations. The unsentimental acceptance or rejection of the limitations or imperfections or differences of these characters (whether attributed to disability, race, crime, religion or sanity) typically underpins her narrative plots. Her posthumously compiled *Complete Stories* won the 1972 U.S. National Book Award for Fiction and remains an American classic. Immensely quotable, her line "The truth does not change according to our ability to stomach it" is still very timely.

6 This posthumous image of Mary Shelley is held at The Bodleian Library, the main research library of the University of Oxford.

[7] Pablo Neruda (July 12, 1904 – September 23, 1973) was a Chilean poet-diplomat and politician who won the 1971 Nobel Prize in Literature. Neruda became known as a poet when he was 13 years old and wrote in a variety of styles, including surrealist poems, historical epics, political manifestos, a prose autobiography, and passionate love poems such as the ones in his collection *Twenty Love Poems and a Song of Despair*.

[8] Camille Paglia (born April 2, 1947) is an American academic and social critic and feminist. A professor at the University of the Arts in Philadelphia, Pennsylvania, since 1984, her work can be wildly controversial. Paglia is critical of many aspects of modern culture and is the author of *Sexual Personae: Art and Decadence from Nefertiti to Emily Dickinson* (1990) and other books.

[9] Rainer Maria Rilke (December 4, 1875 – December 29, 1926), was an idiosyncratic and expressive Austrian poet, widely recognized as a significant writer in the German tradition. His work is viewed by critics and scholars as possessing undertones of mysticism, exploring themes of subjective experience and disbelief.

[10] Etched portraiture of Franz Kafka by printmaker Jan Hladík (1978).

[11] Percy Bysshe Shelley (August 4, 1792 – July 8, 1822) was considered one of the major English Romantic poets. A radical in his poetry as well as in his political and social views, Shelley did not achieve fame during his lifetime, but recognition of his achievements in poetry grew steadily following his demise, and he became a wide-ranging influence on subsequent generations of poets, including Robert Browning, Algernon Charles Swinburne, Thomas Hardy, and W. B. Yeats. Literary critic Harold Bloom describes him as "a superb craftsman, a lyric poet without rival, and surely one of the most advanced sceptical <sic> intellects ever to write a poem." A sculpture near Amarillo, Texas pays homage to Shelley's poem "Ozymandias".

"In 'The Defence of Poetry' 1821, Shelley claimed that 'poets are the unacknowledged legislators of the world'. This has been taken to suggest that simply by virtue of composing verse, they exert some exemplary moral power, in a vague unthreatening way. In fact, in his earlier political essay, 'A Philosophic View of Reform', he had written that 'Poets and philosophers are the unacknowledged', etc. The philosophers, he was talking about, were revolutionary-minded: Thomas Paine, William Godwin, Voltaire and Mary Wollstonecraft.

In addition, Shelley was, no mistake, out to change the legislation of his time. For him, there was no contradiction between poetry, political philosophy and active confrontation with illegitimate authority. For him, art bore an integral relationship to the 'struggle between revolution and oppression'. His 'West Wind' was the 'trumpet of a prophecy', driving 'dead thoughts … like withered leaves, to quicken a new birth'". –from "Legislators of the world" by Adrienne Rich. *Community Development Journal*, Volume 42, Issue 4, October 2007, pp 422–424.

[12] A harsh critic of President Jackson, Ohio Congressman William Stanbery had recently criticized President Andrew Jackson's administration's Indian policy on the House floor and suggested that Sam Houston had conspired with government agents

to defraud the Cherokee Indians while he was the Governor of Tennessee. Houston was incensed by the groundless accusations and subsequently demanded an apology. Houston even went so far as to make overtures regarding a duel, but Stanbery ignored him. Houston confronted Stanbery on Pennsylvania Avenue on April 13, 1832 and, after an argument, struck Stanberry with his cane. Stanbery pulled gun and fired on Houston, but the pistol backfired—which lengthened Stanbery's beating.

[13] Francis Scott Key (August 1, 1779 – January 11, 1843) was an American lawyer, author, and amateur poet from Frederick, Maryland. He is best known as the author of the text of the U.S. national anthem, "The Star-Spangled Banner".

Key had observed the British bombardment of Fort McHenry in 1814 during the War of 1812. He was inspired upon seeing the American flag still standing at dawn and wrote the poem "Defence of Fort M'Henry". It was published within a week with the accompaniment of the popular song "To Anacreon in Heaven". The song and Key's lyrics became known as "The Star-Spangled Banner" and slowly gained in popularity as an unofficial anthem, achieving official status more than a century later under President Herbert Hoover.

[14] University of Texas alumnus Karl Christian Rove (born December 25, 1950) is an American Republican political consultant, policy advisor, and lobbyist. He was Senior Advisor and Deputy Chief of Staff during the George W. Bush administration until his resignation on August 31, 2007. He has also headed the Office of Political Affairs, the Office of Public Liaison, and the White House Office of Strategic Initiatives. Prior to his White House appointments, Rove is credited with the 1994 and 1998 Texas gubernatorial victories of George W. Bush, as well as Bush's successful 2000 and 2004 presidential campaigns. Rove has also been credited for the successful campaigns of John Ashcroft (1994 U.S. Senate election), Bill Clements (1986 Texas gubernatorial election), Senator John Cornyn (2002 U.S. Senate election), Governor Rick Perry (1990 Texas Agriculture Commission election), and Phil Gramm (1982 U.S. House and 1984 U.S. Senate elections).

[15] Barbara Charline Jordan (February 21, 1936 – January 17, 1996) was an American lawyer, educator, and Democratic politician. She was the first African American elected to the Texas Senate after Reconstruction, the first Southern African-American woman elected to the United States House of Representatives, and one of the first two African Americans elected to the U.S. House from the former Confederacy since 1901 (alongside Andrew Young of Georgia).

Jordan achieved notoriety for delivering a powerful opening statement at the House Judiciary Committee hearings during the Nixon impeachment process. In 1976, she became the first woman and the first African American to deliver a keynote address at a Democratic National Convention. She received the Presidential Medal of Freedom in 1994. She was also the first African-American woman to be buried in the Texas State Cemetery—her grave sits near that of the "Father of Texas" Stephen F. Austin.

[16] Katherine Anne Porter (May 15, 1890 – September 18, 1980) was an American journalist, essayist, short story writer, novelist, poet and political activist. Her 1962 novel *Ship of Fools* was the best-selling novel in America that year, but her short stories received much more critical acclaim. Porter was the recipient of many awards, including: the 1966 Pulitzer Prize for Fiction (for *The Collected Stories*); the 1966 National Book Award (for The Collected Stories); and the 1967 Gold Medal Award for Fiction from the American Academy of Arts and Letters. She was also nominated for the Nobel Prize in Literature five times (1964, 1965, 1966, 1967, 1968).

[17] Rosa Louise McCauley Parks (February 4, 1913 – October 24, 2005) is best known for her pivotal role in the Montgomery bus boycott. The United States Congress has honored her as "the first lady of civil rights" and "the mother of the freedom movement". Parks became an NAACP activist in 1943, participating in several high-profile civil rights campaigns. On December 1, 1955, in Montgomery, Alabama, Parks rejected bus driver James F. Blake's instructions to vacate a row of four seats in the "colored" section in favor of a white passenger, once the "white" section was filled. Parks was not the first person to resist bus segregation, but the NAACP considered her the best candidate for seeing through a court challenge after her arrest for civil disobedience in Alabama. Parks subsequently helped inspire the Black community to boycott the Montgomery buses for over a year. The case became bogged down in the state courts, but the federal Montgomery bus lawsuit *Browder v. Gayle* resulted in a November 1956 decision that bus segregation was unconstitutional under the Equal Protection Clause of the 14th Amendment to the U.S. Constitution.

[18] Hermann Karl Hesse (July 2, 1877 – August 9, 1962) was a German-Swiss poet, novelist, and painter. His best-known works include *Demian*, *Steppenwolf*, *Siddhartha*, and *The Glass Bead Game*, each of which explores an individual's search for authenticity, self-knowledge and spirituality. Hesse received the Nobel Prize in Literature in 1946.

[19] Dylan Marlais Thomas (October 27, 1914 – November 9, 1953) was a Welsh poet and writer whose works include the poems "Do not go gentle into that good night" and "And death shall have no dominion." He was widely popular in his lifetime and remained so after his death at the age of thirty-nine in New York City.

Although Thomas wrote exclusively in the English language, he is acknowledged as one of the most important Welsh poets of the 20th century, noted for his original, rhythmic, and ingenious use of words and imagery.

[20] Anne Sexton (born Anne Gray Harvey, November 9, 1928 – October 4, 1974) was an American poet known for her highly personal, confessional verse. She won the Pulitzer Prize for poetry in 1967 for her book *Live or Die*.

[21] Greta Tintin Eleonora Ernman Thunberg (born January 3, 2003) is a Swedish environmental activist known for challenging world leaders to take immediate action for climate change.

[22] Comedian Bill Hicks at the Laff Stop in Austin in the Fall of 1991. Photo by Austin resident Angela Davis.

[23] The Stasi was a secret police agency of the German Democratic Republic (East Germany). The Stasi was one of the most hated and feared institutions of the East German communist government from 1950 - 1990.

[24] The *Geheime Staatspolizei*, abbreviated Gestapo, was the official secret police of Nazi Germany and in Nazi-occupied Europe. The police force was created by Hermann Göring in 1933 by combining the various political police agencies of Prussia into one organization.

[25] Maya Angelou (born Marguerite Annie Johnson, April 4, 1928 – May 28, 2014) was an American memoirist, poet, and civil rights activist. She published seven autobiographies, three books of essays, several books of poetry, and is credited with a list of plays, movies, and television shows spanning over 50 years. She received dozens of awards and more than 50 honorary degrees. Angelou's debut novel, *I Know Why the Caged Bird Sings* (1969), tells the story of her life up to the age of seventeen. It brought her international recognition and critical acclaim.

[26] *Coriolanus* is a tragedy by William Shakespeare, believed to have been written in the early 1600s. The play is based on the life of the legendary Roman leader Caius Marcius Coriolanus. Shakespeare worked on *Coriolanus* simultaneously with *Antony and Cleopatra*, making them his last two tragedies.

Coriolanus was the name given to a Roman general after his military feats against the Volscians at Corioli. After his military successes, he seeks to be consul, but his disdain for the plebeians and mutual hostility with the tribunes lead to his banishment from Rome. Once exiled, he joins the Volscians and leads them against Rome. After he relents and agrees to a peace with Rome, he is killed by his former Volscian allies.

[27] Jacques-Yves Cousteau, (June 11, 1910 – June 25, 1997) was a French naval officer, oceanographer, filmmaker and author. He co-invented the first successful, self-contained underwater breathing apparatus ("SCUBA"), called the Aqua-Lung, which assisted him in producing some of the first underwater documentaries.

Cousteau authored several books describing his undersea explorations. In his first volume, *The Silent World: A Story of Undersea Discovery and Adventure*, Cousteau theorized the existence of the echolocation abilities of porpoises. The book was adapted into an underwater documentary called *The Silent World*. Co-directed by Cousteau and Louis Malle, it was one of the first films to use underwater cinematography to document the ocean depths in color. The film won the 1956 Palme d'Or at the Cannes Film Festival and remained the only documentary to do so until 2004 (when *Fahrenheit 9/11* received the award). It also won the Academy Award for Best Documentary in 1957.

From 1966 to 1976, Cousteau hosted *The Undersea World of Jacques Cousteau*, a documentary television series, broadcasted on American commercial television stations. A second documentary series, *The Cousteau Odyssey*, ran from 1977 to 1982 on public television stations.

[28] According to the United Nations, the world population reached 8 billion on November 15, 2022.

[29] The illustration commented on the urgency and current number of victims of the Spanish Civil War.

[30] *As Good as It Gets* (1997) is a romantic comedy-drama film directed by James L. Brooks, who co-wrote it with Mark Andrus. The film stars Jack Nicholson as a misanthropic, bigoted, and obsessive–compulsive novelist, Helen Hunt as a single mother with a young, chronically ill son, and Greg Kinnear as a homosexual artist. Nicholson and Hunt won the Academy Award for Best Actor and Best Actress.

[31] It's no coincidence that Dick Cheney also worked in the Nixon White House with Roger Ailes and Donald Rumsfeld.

[32] U.S. National Oceanic and Atmospheric Administration.

[33] BP p.l.c. (formerly The British Petroleum Company p.l.c. and BP Amoco p.l.c., stylized bp) is a British multinational oil and gas company headquartered in London, England. It is an oil and gas "supermajor" and one of the world's largest companies measured by revenues and profits. It operates in all areas of the oil and gas industry, including exploration and extraction, refining, distribution and marketing, power generation, and trading.

[34] Attributed on Wikipedia Commons to takomabibelot.

[35] Part of the Musée Antoine-Lécuyer collection in Saint-Quentin, France.

[36] Sorry, I couldn't resist. "Wango Tango" is a song written and recorded by conservative American rocker Ted Nugent. It peaked on the Billboard Hot 100 at #86 in 1980, and has been a staple of Nugent's live performances for many years.

[37] A rat race is a ceaseless, self-defeating, or pointless pursuit. The term equates humans to rats futilely attempting to earn a reward, such as cheese. It also refers to the struggle to get ahead financially. The phrase is commonly associated with an exhausting, repetitive lifestyle that leaves no time for relaxation or enjoyment.

The dates back to 1934, In reference to an aviation training exercise dubbed a "rat race" because a trainee fighter pilot had to copy all the actions (loops, rolls, spins, turns, etc. performed by an experienced pilot. From 1945 on, the phrase took on the meaning of "competitive struggle."

[38] In the January 31, 2014 *Psychology Today* article, "The Lloyd Dobler Effect", Camille S. Johnson, PhD., observes that "The magic of the movie [*Say Anything*] was in Lloyd's pursuit of Diane. He took her to parties, taught her to drive, and when she broke up with him, stood outside her room, in the now-legendary stance, with a boombox playing 'In Your Eyes' [by Peter Gabriel]. This movie has been called the Ultimate Chickflick, so it might be easy to see how women were affected by it. One could imagine that we spent the '90s looking for a gentle (yet strong), smart (yet humble), man who would stand outside our windows with Peter Gabriel expressing his thoughts", that "we looked for a man who would follow us as we pursued our goals and ambitions, and who would support us in our aspirations. And, Lloyd Dobler from the middle-class Midwest was the ultimate example. Of course, compared to fictional Lloyd, what man could compare?" Johnson's article comments on the unrealist expectations the "Dobler" character led to. "Indeed, once the behaviors of

Lloyd become ingrained in our definitions of what makes a good partner, we may forget the movie and forget the source, and the definition becomes automatic. In this way, John Cusack's Lloyd Dobler, Judd Nelson's John Bender, Matthew Broderick's Ferris Bueller, shape people's views of an ideal (and possible) romantic partner."

[39] Peele's *Candyman* was a remake. The original was a 1992 American gothic horror film, written and directed by Bernard Rose and starring Xander Berkeley, Kasi Lemmons, Virginia Madsen, Tony Todd, and Vanessa E. Williams. Based on Clive Barker's short story "The Forbidden", a Chicago graduate student working to complete a thesis on urban legends and folklore, examines the legend of the "Candyman", the ghost of an African American artist and the son of a slave who was murdered in the late 19th century for his relationship with a wealthy white man's daughter. The *Philadelphia Inquirer* called the original *Candyman* "A rare horror film that has something to say."

[40] Some reports indicate several captured Black Union soldiers were burned alive at Camp Ford in Tyler, Texas.

[41] Daily News Leader (Staunton, Virginia), May 22, 1988.

[42] Michael Hurd is the former director of Prairie View A&M University's Texas Institute for the Preservation of History and Culture, which documents the history of African American Texans. He has worked as a sports writer for the *Houston Post*, the *Austin American-Statesman*, *USA Today*, and *Yahoo Sports*. He is the author of *Thursday Night Lights* (2017).

[43] The Great Hanging was the execution forty-one suspected Unionists in Gainesville, Texas, in October 1862, during the American Civil War. Confederate troops shot two additional suspects trying to escape. Confederate troops captured and arrested some 150–200 men in the Cooke County area at a time when numerous North Texas citizens opposed the new Confederate conscription law. Many suspects were tried by a "Citizens' Court" organized by a Confederate military officer. It made up its own rules for conviction and had no status under state law. Although only eleven percent of county households owned slaves, seven of the twelve men on the jury were slaveowners. The suspects were executed one or two at a time.

[44] In the early afternoon of Wednesday, January 6, 2021, two months after the defeat of 45th U.S. president Donald Trump in the 2020 presidential election, a mob of his supporters attacked the United States Capitol Building in Washington, D.C. The mob sought to keep Trump in power by preventing a joint session of Congress from affirming the Electoral College votes to formalize the victory of President-elect Joe Biden. According to the House select committee that investigated the incident, the attack was the culmination of a seven-part plan by Donald Trump to overturn the 2020 presidential election results.

[45] This column appeared in my previous collection of editorials, *Fear and Loathing in the Lone Star State* (2021).

[46] A modus operandi is a particular way or method of doing something, especially

one that is characteristic or well-established.

[47] A glaring example of this is the recent removal of books on slavery from plantation museum gift shops by the new, conservative incarnation of the Texas Historical Commission. An agency spokesperson, however, told *Texas Monthly* the move had nothing to do with politics.

[48] The Fairness Doctrine of the U. S. Federal Communications Commission (FCC), introduced in 1949, was a policy that required the holders of broadcast licenses both to present controversial issues of public importance and to do so in a manner that fairly reflected differing viewpoints. In 1987, the FCC abolished the Fairness Doctrine, prompting many to urge its reintroduction through either Commission policy or congressional legislation. In response, the FCC removed the rule that implemented the policy from the Federal Register in August 2011.

The Fairness Doctrine was comprised of two basic elements: (1) it required broadcasters to devote some of their airtime to discussing controversial matters of public interest; and (2) it required broadcasters to air contrasting views regarding those matters. Stations were granted wide latitude as to how to present contrasting views—it could be done through news segments, public affairs shows, or editorials. The doctrine did not require equal time for opposing views but required that contrasting viewpoints be presented. The demise of Fairness Doctrine has often been cited as a contributing factor in the rising level of party polarization in the United States.

[49] *Beavis and Butt-Head* is an American *adult* animated sitcom created by Mike Judge for MTV (seasons 1–8) and later Paramount+ (season 9–present, as *Mike Judge's Beavis and Butt-Head*). The series—based in "Highland, Texas"—follows Beavis and Butt-Head, both voiced by Judge, a pair of teenage slackers characterized by their apathy, lack of intelligence, lowbrow humor, and love for hard rock and heavy metal.

During its initial run, *Beavis and Butt-Head* received critical acclaim for its asinine, satirical, scathing commentary on society, as well as criticism for its alleged influence on adolescents. It produced various other media, including the theatrical film *Beavis and Butt-Head Do America* in 1996. A second film, *Beavis and Butt-Head Do the Universe*, was released in 2022 on Paramount+. *Image courtesy of Gage Skidmore from Surprise, Arizona*

[50] Alexis Charles Henri Clérel, comte de Tocqueville (July 29, 1805 – April 16, 1859), was a French aristocrat, diplomat, sociologist, political scientist, political philosopher, and historian. Tocqueville is best known for his works *Democracy in America* (appearing in two volumes, 1835 and 1840) and *The Old Regime and the Revolution* (1856). In both, he analyzed the living standards and social conditions of individuals as well as their relationship to the market and state in Western societies. *Democracy in America* was published after Tocqueville's travels in the United States. Today, it is considered an important early work of sociology and political science.

[51] Silver gelatin photograph in the Argus Newspaper Collection of Photographs, State Library of Victoria. Image circa 1941.

[52] The Christchurch Mosque shootings were two consecutive murder sprees on two mosques in Christchurch, New Zealand on March 15, 2019. The mass shootings were committed by Brenton Tarrant. He two mosques during Friday prayer, the Al Noor Mosque at 1:40 p.m. and later at the Linwood Islamic Centre at 1:52 p.m.

Tarrant was arrested after his vehicle was rammed by a police unit as he was driving to a third mosque in Ashburton. He was described in media reports as a white supremacist. He had live-streamed the first shooting on Facebook and had published an online manifesto before the attacks.

On March 26 2020, he pleaded guilty to fifty-one murders, forty attempted murders, and engaging in a terrorist act. In August 2020 Tarrant was sentenced to life imprisonment without the possibility of parole—the first life sentence in New Zealand.

[53] The Great Replacement, also known as replacement theory or great replacement theory, is a far-right, white nationalist conspiracy theory espoused by French author Renaud Camus. The original theory claims that, with the cooperation of "replacist" elites, the ethnic French and white European populations at large are being demographically and culturally replaced by non-white peoples—especially from Muslim-majority countries—through mass migration, demographic growth and a drop in the birth rate of white Europeans. Scholars dismiss the theory for being based on a basic misunderstanding of demographic statistics and rooted in blatant racism and general xenophobia.

www.ingramcontent.com/pod-product-compliance
Lightning Source LLC
Chambersburg PA
CBHW071323140726
47996CB00005B/1796